IRISH LAND AND CONVEYANCING LAW

by
DENIS M. LINEHAN
Solicitor, A.C.I. Arb., Former Fellow
of Salzburg Seminar (Austria), B.C.L. (N.U.I.),
LL.M. (Univ. of Mich), LL.M. (Harvard),
Consultant.

To my son, Denis

EMERALD PUBLICATIONS LTD.

1995

Published by Emerald Publications Ltd.

Emerald books are available at selected bookstores or can be ordered direct in Ireland through:-
Copy Design Bureau, 20 Denroches Cross, Glasheen Road, Cork.
Tel: (021) 310876   Fax: (021) 310983

First published:1989
Second edition:1995

Cover illustration: Teresa Power

Paperback   ISBN 0-9525813-8-8
Hardback   ISBN 0-9525813-3-7

Printed and bound in the European Union

Preface

This book, when initially published in 1989, represented the first contemporary effort to include Irish Land and Conveyancing Law in a single volume. The book divides into four parts. The first two treat of traditional areas of land law and conveyancing law, respectively. The third part covers important legislation pertinent to the first two. The final part consists of Appendices on law arising in most conveyancing transactions.

Those who are expert and experienced in land and conveyancing law will know that each of the areas dealt with is the subject of at least one specialist reference book. Nonetheless, I believe that such readers will find this book useful.

At the other end of the spectrum of readers, one envisages the student of the subject. For such, it is thought that the book presents the subject in a manner uncluttered by analysis or elaboration.

The ambition of the book, it is hoped, is clear from the preceding remarks. It is not intended as a reference book with a capital "R". Neither is it intended as a basic introduction to the subject. Rather, it is intended to present mainstream precepts of land and conveyancing law in a form convenient and concise.

Since the first edition of the book was published in 1989, there have been a number of significant changes in the law that are referred to in this edition. Thus, first, two new statutes bearing on Leasehold Interests have been enacted, namely, the Landlord and Tenant (Amendment) Acts of 1989 and 1994. The 1989 statute has very limited scope, and bears only on the statutory rights of a tenant or lessee of a tenement in the Custom House Docks Area of Dublin. The 1994 statute has made a small number of minor modifications to the Landlord and Tenant (Amendment) Act, 1980. Probably the most important of these is the alteration of the qualifications for the "business equity" under section 13(1)(a) of the earlier statute by the extension of the requisite period of occupation from three to five years in respect of a lease or other contract of tenancy that begins to run after the commencement of the later Act.

Secondly, a new standard Contract of Sale was introduced in 1991 by the Incorporated Law Society of Ireland in place of the previous 1988 edition. Thirdly, a number of developments have occured that bear on the chapter entitled "Consents Required under the Land Act, 1965". Most notably, the Land Commission was disolved by the Irish Land Commission (Dissolution) Act, 1992, and its functions were re-allocated between the High Court and the Minister for Agriculture and Food. In addition, the categories of "qualified persons" within the meaning of section 45 of the Land Act, 1965, have been expanded by two statutory instruments of 1994 and 1995. S.I. No. 67 of 1994 has created a new such category, namely, a person acquiring an interest in land situate within the Counties of Dublin South, Fingal and Dun Laoghaire- Rathdown as specified in the Local Government (Dublin) Act, 1993.

S.I. No. 56 of 1995 has also added to the list of qualified persons. These now also include persons whose principal place of residence is in a Member State of the European Communities or in any other European State which is a contracting party to the European Economic Area Agreement and bodies corporate incorporated, having their registered office, central administration or principal place of business in those States.

Fourthly, a number of changes have occurred in relation to Stamp Duties by virtue of the Finance Acts passed since 1989. Some of the more significant changes are noted in Appendix A.

In concluding these prefatory remarks I wish to thank all those who helped me bring this second edition of the book to publication.

Denis M. Linehan
October, 1995

Contents

Preface .... *Page* vii
Table of Cases xv
Table of Statutes xxi

Part One – Land Law

1. Nature of Real Property 3
Real Property and Personal Property Contrasted 3
Special Classification of Leaseholds 3
Differences Arising from the Distinction Between Real
and Personal Property 4
Tenure 4

2. Freehold Estates 6
Introduction 6
Fee Simple 6
Fee Tail 10
Base Fee 12
Life Estate 12
Rights of Holder of Life Estate 14

3. Leasehold Interests 16
Introduction 16
Relationship of Landlord and Tenant Based on Contract . 17
Formalities Necessary in Creating the Relationship 18
Contents of the Contract 20
Types of Leasehold Interests 20
Rent 24
Repairs 26
User of Demised Property 28
Alterations to, and Improvements of, Demised Property . 29
Insurance of Demised Property 29
Alienation of Demised Property 29

Covenants to Yield up Possession 30
Landlord's Obligations to Tenant 30
Determination of Leasehold Interests 31

4. Co-Ownership 37
Introduction 37
Joint Tenancy and Tenancy in Common 38
Characteristics 38
Preference for One Form of Co-Ownership over Another   39
Consequences of Different Types of Co-Ownership 40
Coparcenary 43
Tenancy by Entireties 43
Family Home Protection Act, 1976 44

5. Future Interests 45
Introduction 45
Vested and Contingent Interests 46
Types of Future Interests 47
Rules Governing the Validity of Legal Remainders 53
Rules Governing the Remoteness of Vesting of
Future Interests 55
Rule in *Whitby* v. *Mitchell* 56
Rule against Perpetuities 56
Rule against Perpetual Trusts 61
Rule against Accumulation of Income 63
Rule in *Shelley*'s Case 64

6. Mortgages 65
Mortgage Defined 65
Importance of the Mortgage in Conveyancing Practice ... 65
Creation of Mortgages 68
Legal Mortgages 68
Equitable Mortgages 70
Mortgagee's Rights, Powers and Remedies 72
Mortgagor's Rights, Powers and Remedies 80
Priority Between Mortgages 82
Judgement Mortgages 83

7. Easements and Profits 85
Easement Defined 85
Prerequisites to Easements 85
Acquisition of Easements 86

The Easement of Light 92
Relationship Between Dominant and Servient Owners . 94
Extinguishment of Easements 95
Profits A Prendre 96
Acquisition of Profits 97
Extinguishment of Profits 98

8. **Succession** 99
    Introduction 99
    Beneficial Devolution of Realty on Intestacy
    before the Succession Act 100
    Determining Degrees of Kinship 103
    Beneficial Devolution of Personalty on Intestacy
    before the Succession Act 105
    Advancements 108
    Intestates' Estate Acts, 1890 and 1954 108
    Beneficial Devolution of All Property on Intestacy
    after the Succession Act 109
    Various Aspects of the Law Relating to Wills 111
    Power of Testation 115

Part Two – Conveyancing Law

9. **Stages in a Conveyance** 123
    Introduction 123
    First Stage: From Preliminary Negotiations to Contract   123
    Second Stage: From Contract to Closing 124
    Third Stage: Closing 126
    Fourth Stage: After Closing 126

10. **The Contract of Sale** 128
    Types of Contract 128
    Compliance of Contract of Sale with Statute of Frauds   129
    Relationship Arising Between Vendor and Purchaser
    Under the Contract of Sale 131
    Discharge of the Contract 135
    Enforcement of the Contract of Sale 135

11. **The Standard Contract of Sale** 139
    Introduction 139
    Preliminary 139
    Consent of Spouse and Memorandum of Agreement .. 139

Particulars and Tenure 140
Schedules of Documents and Searches 141
Special Conditions 142
General Conditions of Sale 143

12. Title to be Shown Under an Open Contract 155
Introduction 155
Searching Title to Unregistered Freehold Property 155
Searching Title to Unregistered Leasehold Property 157
Bad Roots of Title. Vendor's Duty of Disclosure 160

13. Consents Required under the Land Act, 1965 161
Introduction 161
Section 12, Land Act, 1965 161
Section 45, Land Act, 1965 164

**14. Form and Effect of a Conveyance
of a Fee Simple**   169
The Deed as a Conveyancing Instrument 169
Meaning of Conveyance 169
Form of a Conveyance of a Fee Simple 169
Covenants for Title 175
Practice after Completion 177

15. Agency and Conveyancing   183
Creation of Agency 183
Agency by Authority 183
Agency by Ratification 184
Agency of Necessity 186
Relationship between Principal and Agent 186
Duties of an Agent 186
Rights of an Agent 188
Relationship of Principal and Agent to Third Parties ... 191
Termination of Agency 196
Auctioneers and Estate Agents 198

**Part Three – Legislation on Land and
Conveyancing Law**

16. Settled Land Acts 203
Introduction 203
Settled Land Defined 204

Tenant for Life 204
Powers of a Tenant For Life 205
Trustees of the Settlement 208
Overreaching 211

17. **Registration of Deeds** 214
Introduction 214
Registrable Documents 215
Method of Registration 215
Rules Governing Priorities 216
Records Maintained in the Registry of Deeds 217
Searches in the Registry of Deeds 218

18. **Registration of Title** 220
Introduction 220
Land Registry Offices and Registers 221
Classes of Ownership in the Land Registry 223
Classes of Title that may be Registered 224
Conclusiveness of the Register 227
Compulsory Registration 228
First Registration 230
Land Registry Transfers 230
Cautions and Inhibitions 231
Land Registry Searches 233
Land Certificate 234

Part Four – Appendices on Land and Conveyancing Law

APPENDIX A: Stamp Duty 237
Introduction 237
Ad Valorem Duty 237
Fixed Rate of Duty 240
General Exemptions from Stamp Duty 241

APPENDIX B: Subsidiary Searches in Conveyancing Transactions 242
Introduction 242
Freehold Property 242
Leasehold Property 243
Subsidiary Searches for both Freehold and Leasehold Property 244

APPENDIX C: Impact of the Family Home Protection Act, 1976, and the Family Law Act, 1981 245

    Family Home Protection Act, 1976 245

    Family Law Act, 1981 247

INDEX 249

Table of Cases

Annally Hotel Ltd. v. Bergin [1970] 1 I.L.T.R. 6 87
Annesley v. Rooney 18 I.L.T.R. 100 24

Bailey v. Appleyard [1839] 8 A. & E. 161 89
Bank of Ireland v. Domvile [1956] I.R. 37 11
Bank of Ireland v. Waldrow [1944] I.R. 303 .... 74, 75, 132
Barclay's Bank v. Breen 96 I.L.T.R. 179 195
Barden v. Downes [1940] I.R. 131 .... 73, 75
Binions v. Evans [1972] Ch. 359 22
Bradley v. Carritt [1903] A.C. 253 82
Breaden v. Fuller & Son Ltd. [1949] I.R. 290 35
Brennan v. O'Connell and Another [1975] Unrep.
[Sup. Ct., I.R.] [1974 No. 8] 130
Browne v. Burton [1847] 17 L.J., Q.B. 49 170
Browne v. Maguire [1922] 1 I.R. 23 88
Browne v. Ryan [1901] 2 I.R. 653 81
Bruce v. Brophy [1906] 1 I.R. 611 75
Bryant v. Foot [1868] I.R. 3 Q.B. 497 89
Byrne v. Byrne [1953] 87 I.L.T.R. 183 61

Calvert, Re [1898] 2 I.R. 501 79
Cardigan v. Curzon-Howe [1885] 30 Ch.D. 531 205
Caulfield v. Farr I.R. 7 C.L. 469 23
Cheese v. Lovejoy [1877] 2 P.D. 251 115
Cleary v. Bohen [1931] L.J. I.R. 148 94
Cloncurry v. Laffan [1924] I.R. 78 130
Cochrane v. Verner [1895] 29 I.L.J. 571 86
Cockerill v. Gilliland [1854] 6 Ir. Jur. [O.S.] 357 ...... 38, 41
Coghlan, Re [1963] I.R. 246 9
Colls v. Home and Colonial Stores Ltd. [1904] A.C. 179 93
Convey v. Regan [1952] I.R. 56 97
Connolly v. Connolly [1866] 17 I.R. Ch.R. 208 41
Corkerry v. Stack 82 I.L.T.R. 60 25

Costelloe v. Maharaj Krishna Properties [Ire] Ltd. Unrep.
[1975] [H.C., R.I.] [1974 No. 1564 P] 138
Cowan v. Factor [1948] I.R. 128 .... 27, 28
Crickmore v. Freeston [1870] 40 L.J. Ch. 137 81
Curoe v. Gordon 26 I.L.T.R. 95 32
Cusack v. Farrell, 18 L.R. Ir. 494 23

Daniel v. Vassall, Re Daniel [1971] 2 Ch. 405 133
Davies v. Marshall [1861] 10 C.B. [N.S.] 697 95
De Sommery, Re [1912] 2 Ch. 622 60
Dean, Re [1889] 41 Ch.D. 552 62
Doherty v. Gallagher [1975] Unrep. [H.C., R.I.]
[1973 No. 2830 P] 138
Donnelly v. Adams [1905] 1 I.R. 157 88
Dyas v. Stafford [1871] 7 L.R. Ir. 590 199

Edgar, Re [1939] 1 All E.R. 635 9
Ewart's Estate, Re [1967] 18 N.I.L.Q. 463 59
Exham v. Beamish [1939] I.R. 336 58
Eyre v. McDowell [1861] 9 H.L.C. 619 70

Fairclough v. Swan Brewery Co. Ltd. [1912] A.C. 565 81
Fulmerston v. Steward [1596] Cro. Jac. 592 52
Fleming v. Brennan [1941] I.R. 499 28
Fleming v. Fleming [1855] 5 I.R. Ch.R. 129 40
Flood's Estate, Re [1862] 13 Ir. Ch.R. 312 217
Flynn v. Flynn [1930] I.R. 337 41
Flynn v. Harte [1913] 2 I.R. 322 90
Frewen v. Relfe [1787] 2 Bro. C.C. 220 41

Gannon v. Hughes [1937] I.R. 284 93
Gardner v. Hodgson's Kingston Brewery Co. Ltd.
[1903] A.C. 229 91
Gaw v. C.I.E. [1953] I.R. 232 94
Gilbourne v. Gilbourne, Re [1975] Unrep. [H.C., R.I.] 64
Gilligan v. National Bank Ltd. [1901] 2 I.R. 513 79
Gore-Hickman v. Alliance Assurance Co. Ltd. [1936] I.R. 721   80
Gowrie Park Utility Society Ltd. v. Fitzgerald [1963] I.R. 436 23
Griffin v. Keane [1927] 61 I.L.T.R. 177 95

Harris v. Swordy [1975] Unrep. [H.C., R.I.] 134
Hawkesworth's Estate, Re [1878] 1 L.R. I.R. 179 43

Hawkins v. Rogers [1951] I.R. 48 40
Hawkins v. Rutter [1892] 1 Q.B. 668 86
Healy v. Healy [1973] Unrep. [H.C., R.I.] 138
Hedley Byrne and Co. Ltd. v. Heller and Partners Ltd.
[1963] 2 All E.R. 575 187
Henehan v. Courtney and Hanley 101 I.L.T.R. 25 190
Hill v. Tupper [1863] 2 H. & C. 121 86
Howard v. Maitland [1883] 11 Q.B.D. 695 175
Hurley v. Hurley [1908] 1 I.R. 393 33
Hyman v. Van Den Bergh [1907] 2 Ch. 500 93

Irish Welding Co. Ltd. v. Philips Electrical (Ireland) Ltd.
[1976] Unrep. [H.C., R.I.] [1974 No. 3565P] 196

James Calvert, Re [1898] 2 I.R. 501 79
James H. North Ltd. v. Dinan [1931] I.R. 486 189
Jameson v. McGovern [1934] I.R. 758 7

Kavanagh v. Cuthbert [1874] I.R. 9 C.L. 136 199
Keighley, Maxsted & Co. v. Durant [1901] A.C. 240 185
Kelly, Re [1932] I.R. 255 .... 57, 63
Kelly v. Dea [1966] 100 I.L.T.R. 1 .... 94, 95
Kelly v. Park Hall School [1979] I.R. 340 136
Kennedy v. Ryan [1938] I.R. 62O 40
Killner v. France [1946] 2 All E.R. 83 135
Knightbridge Estates T. Ltd. v. Byrne [1939] Ch. 441 (C.A.)   81
Knight Sugar Co. Ltd. v. Alberta Railway & Irrigation Co.
[1938] 1 All E.R. 266 135
Kreglinger v. New Patagonia Meat & Cold Storage Co. Ltd.
[1914] A.C. 25 82

Law v. Roberts and Co. (Ireland) Ltd. [1964]
I.R. 292 .... 131, 184, 200
Lawrence v. Jenkins [1873] L.R. 8 A.B. 244 94
Lurcott v. Wakely and Wheeler [1911] 1 K.B. 905 28
Lloyd v. Grace, Smith & Co. [1912] A.C. 716 192
Lloyd's Bank Ltd. v. Dalton [1942] 2 A.E.R. 352 96

MacKensie v. Duke of Devonshire [1896] A.C. 400 171
Maguire v. Armstrong [1814] 2 Ba. and B. 538 176
Mansfield, Re [1962] I.R. 454 .... 46, 47

Marsh and Earl Glanville, Re 24 Ch.D. 11 160
Martin v. Mc Causland [1842] 4 Ir. L.R. 340 46
McDonagh v. Mulholland [1931] I.R. 110 88
McDonnell, Re [1965] I.R. 354 61
McDonnell v. Jebb [1865] 16 Ir. Ch.R. 359 39
McGrath v. Munster & Leinster Bank Ltd. [1959] I.R. 313 .. 94
McIlvenny v. McKeever [1931] N.I. 161 33
McMeekin v. Stevenson [1917] I.R. 348 199
Moore, Re [1888] Ch.D. 116 10
Moore v. Rawson [1824] 3 B. & C. 32 96
Munster and Leinster Bank Ltd. v. McGlashan [1937] I.R. 525 133
Murdoch hownie Ltd. v. Newman [1949] 2 All E.R. 783 ... 189
Murphy & Co. Ltd. v. Marren [1933] I.R. 393 77
Murphy, Buckley and Keogh Ltd. v. Pye (Ireland) Ltd.
[1971] I. R. 57 189
Murphy v. Quality Homes [1976] Unrep. [H.C., R.I.]
[1975 No. 4344P] 133

National Bank v. McGovern [1931] I.R. 368 71
National Bank v. Shanahan [1932] 66 I.L.T.R. 120 .... 73, 74
Neaverson v. Peterborough R.D.C. [1902] 1 Ch. 557 97
Nixon v. Darby I.R. 2 C.L. 467 23
Northern Bank Co. Ltd. v. Carpenter [1931] I.R. 268 71

O'Connell v. Harrison [1927] I.R. 330 40
O'Connell v. O'Callaghan [1841] Lory & Town 157 15
O'Flaherty v. Arvan Properties Ltd. [1977] Unrep.
[Sup. Ct., R.I.] 137
O'Reilly v. Gleeson [1975] Unrep. [Sup. Ct., R.I.] 34

Parfitt v. Hember [1867] L.R. 4 Eq. 443 56
Patman v. Harland [1881] 17 Ch.D. 353 .... 158, 159
Pearce v. Morris [1869] 5 Ch. App. 227 81
Petty v. Styward [1632] 2 Ch. Rep. 57 40
Phillips v. Butler [1945] 2 All E.R. 285 131
Poe, Re [1942] I.R. 535 59
Polhill v. Walter [1832] 3 B. and Ad. 114 193
Proudfoot v. Hart 25 Q.B.D. 42 28
Purefoy v. Rogers [1671] 2 Wms. Saund. 380 55

Radcliff v. Hayes [1907] 1 I.R. 101 97

Regis Property Co. Ltd. v. Dudley [1959] A.C. 370 28
Robson, Re [1940] Ir. Jur. Rep. 72 40
R. v. Inhabitants of Hermitage [1692] Carth 239 96

Salt v. Marquess of Northåmpton [1892] A.C. 1 68
Sambach v. Dalston [1634] Tothill 168 50
Shelley's Case [1581] 1 Co. Rep. 88b. 64
Sheridan v. Higgins [1971] I.R. 291 199
Shields v. Shields [1904] 38 I.L.T.R. 188 73
Shinner v. Harman [1853] 31 C.L.R. 243 15
Sichel v. Mosenthal [1862] 30 Beav. 371 70
Smallman Ltd. v. Castle [1932] I.R. 294 25
Smith v. Baxter [1900] 2 Ch. 138 93
Smith v. Chichester [1848] 12 Ir. Eq. R. 519 33
Smith v. Dublin Theatre Co. [1936] I.R. 692 93
Smith v. Smith [1891] 3 Ch. 550 81
Somers v. Nicholls [1955] I.R. 83 190
Stevenson v. Parke [1932] L.J. I.R. 228 95
Sturgeon v. Wingfield [1846] 15 M. & W. 244 24
Siney v. Corporation of Dublin [1980] I.R. 400 27

Tallon v. Ennis [1937] I.R. 549 85
Taylor v. Bydall [1677] 1 Freem. K.B. 24 52
Taylor's Trusts, Re [1912] 1 I.R. 1. 59
Tempany v. Hynes [1976] I.R. 101 132
Timmins v. Moreland Street Property Co. Ltd. [1958] Ch. 110 130
Tisdall v. McArthur & Co. (S. & M.) Ltd. [1951] I.R. 228 89
Tiverton Estates Ltd. v. Wearwell Ltd. [1974] 1 All E.R. 209   136
Turner v. Morgan [1803] 8 Ver. 143 42
Turner v. Moon [1901] 2 Ch. 825 176
Tyrrel's Case [1557] 2 Dyer 155a 49

Vane v. Bernard [1716] 2 Vern 738 15

Walsh v. Lonsdale [1882] 21 Ch. D. 9 19
Wallace v. Daly & Co. Ltd. [1949] I.R. 352 34
Ward and Fegan v. Spivack Ltd. [1957] I.R. 40 197
Westropp v. Congested Districts Bd. [1919] 1 I.R. 224 97
Wheeldon v. Burrows [1879] 12 Ch. D. 31 88
Wheelwright v. Walker [1883] 23 Ch.D. 752 205
Whitby v. Mitchell [1890] 44 Ch. D. 85 56

White v. City of London Brewery Co. [1889] 42 Ch. D. 237 .   74
White v. McCooey [1976] Unrep. [H.C., R.I.]   134
Wilson v. Finch Hatton 2 Ex.D. 336   27
Witty, Re [1913] 2 Ch. 666   60
Wright v. Tracey I.R. 8 C.L. 478   31

Table of Statutes

1217 Magna Carta (18 John) 5, 101
1285 Statute of Westminster II (13 Edw. 1) 10
1290 Statute of Westminster III (Quia Emptores)
     (18 Edw. 1, cc. 1–2) 5
1535 Statutes of Uses (27 Hen. 8, c. 10) 112, 169
1540 Statute of Wills (32 Hen. 8, c. 1) 112
1634 Statutes of Uses (Ireland) (10 Chas 1, sess. 2, c. 1) . 49, 169
1662 Tenures Abolition Act (14 & 15 Chas. 2, sess. 4, c. 19) .. 5
1670 Statute of Distributions 104
1695 Statute of Frauds (Ireland)
     (7 Will. 3, c. 12) 19, 87, 128, 130, 131, 137, 140
     s. 2 .... 18, 70, 129
1707 Registration of Deeds Act (Ireland) (6 Ann. c. 2) 83
     s. 1 215
     s. 3 215
     s. 4 .... 214, 217
     s. 5 .... 216, 217
     s. 6 .... 215, 216
     s. 7 .... 178, 215
     s. 8 218
     s. 14 .... 215, 217
1779 Tenantry Act (19 & 20 Geo. 3, c. 30) 21
     s. 1 21
1832 Prescription Act (2 & 3 Will. 4, c. 71)
     s. 1 90
     s. 2 90
     s. 7 90
     s. 8 90
1832 Registry of Deeds (Ireland) Act (2 & 3 Will. 4, c. 87)
     s. 29 .... 178, 215, 218
     s. 32 214
1833 Real Property Limitation Act (3 & 4 Will. 4, c. 27)
     s. 4 55

s. 5 55
s. 39 55
1833 Dower Act (3 & 4 Will. 4, c. 105) 103
1834 Fines and Recoveries (Ireland) Act (4 & 5 Will. 4, c. 92) . 11
1845 Real Property Act (8 & 9 Vict., c. 106) 169
s. 3 42
s. 8 55
1846 Ejectment and Distress (Ireland) Act (9 & 10 Vict., c. 111)
s. 10 26
s. 14 26
1849 Renewable Leasehold Conversion Act (12 & 13 Vict.,
c. 105) 21
s. 37 8
1850 Judgement Mortgage (Ireland) Act (13 & 14 Vict., c. 29) . 30
s. 6 83
1858 Prescription (Ireland) Act (21 & 22 Vict., c. 42) . 89, 90, 91
s. 3 92
1860 Landlord and Tenant Law Amendment Act, Ireland
(23 & 24 Vict. C. 154) 19
s. 1 28
s. 3 .... 18, 24
s. 4 19
s. 5 22
s. 8 32
s. 9 30
s. 12 24
s. 15 24
s. 20 26
s. 21 26
s. 25 27
s. 39 27
s. 40 .... 25, 32
s. 41 31
s. 42 .... 26, 27
s. 43 34
s. 44 32
s. 45 25
s. 47 25
s. 52 36
s. 72 36
s. 76 25

s. 78 36
1860 Land Purchase Act 220, 221, 227, 229
1867 Sale of Land by Auction Act (30 & 31 Vict., c. 48) 199
1868 Partition Act (31 & 32 Vict., c. 40) 42
1870 Apportionment Act (33 & 34 Vict., c. 35)
s. 2 25
1874 Vendor and Purchaser Act (37 & 38 Vict., c. 78) 155
s. 1 .... 156, 157, 158
s. 2 .... 144, 158
s. 9 134
1876 Notice to Quit (Ireland) Act (39 & 40 Vict., c. 63) 31
1876 Partition Act (39 & 40 Vict., c. 17) 42
1877 Contingent Remainders Act (40 & 41 Vict., c. 33) .. 54, 55
1881 Conveyancing Act (44 & 45 Vict., c. 41) 35, 172
s. 3(1) 144, 159
s. 7(1)(a) 175
s. 13(1) 159
s. 14(1) 34, 35
s. 14(2) 35
s. 16(1) 79
s. 17 79
s. 18 77
s. 19 .... 74, 78
s. 19(1) 76
s. 20 76
s. 23(1) 78
s. 24 76
s. 24(3) 76
s. 24(8) 76
s. 51 .... 7, 11
s. 56 195
s. 65(1) 21
1882 Married Womens' Property Act (45 & 46 Vict., c. 75)
s. 1 44
s. 5 44
1882 Settled Land Act (45 & 46 Vict., c. 38) 203, 210, 224
s. 2 .... 207, 208
s. 2(3) 204

s. 3 205
s. 4(1) 205
s. 5 211
s. 6 206
s. 7 207
s. 10 206
s. 18 207
s. 20 .... 205, 211, 212
s. 22 .... 210, 211, 212
s. 22(2) 210
s. 25 205
s. 26 208
s. 38(1) 209
s. 40 211
s. 42 210
s. 45 205
s. 46(2) 212
s. 49(2) 207
s. 50 205
s. 53 204
s. 58(1) 204
1890 Settled Land Act (53 & 55 Vict., c. 69) 203, 210, 224
s. 10 210
s. 12 211
s. 13 208
s. 15 208
s. 16 209
s. 26 211
1890 Intestates' Estates Act (53 & 54 Vict.,
c. 29) 106, 107, 108, 109
s. 1 109
1891 Local Registration of Title (IR.) Act (54 & 55 Vict.,
c. 66) 220
1891 Stamp Act (54 & 55 Vict., c. 39) 173
s. 15(2) 170
s. 59 240
s. 75 239
1892 Conveyancing Act (55 & 56 Vict., c. 13) 35
s. 4 35
1892 Accumulations Act 63
1901 Land Purchase Act 220, 227, 229

1903 Irish Land Act (3 Edw. 7, c. 37) 164
1908 Law of Distress Amendment Act (8 Edw. 7, c. 53)
     ss. 1-5 26
1911 Conveyancing Act (1 & 2 Geo. 5, c. 37) 74
     s. 3 78
1912 Criminal Law Amendment Act
     s. 5(1) 29
1927 Intoxicating Liquor Act (No. 15)
     s. 51 32
1942 Central Bank Act (No. 22) 166, 182
1947 Auctioneers and House Agents Act (No. 10) 199
1950 Land Act (No. 16) 164
1954 Intestates' Estates Act (No. 12) 106, 107, 108, 109
     ss. 3–5 109
1957 Statute of Limitations Act (No. 6) 80, 96, 228, 234
1957 Married Womens' Status Act (No. 5)
     s. 12 248
1959 Administration of Estates Act (No. 8) 109
1963 Companies Act (No. 33) 165
     s. 37 185
1963 Local Government (Planning and Development) Act
     (No. 28) 7, 29, 116, 243
1964 Registration of Title Act (No. 16) 141, 156
     s. 7 221
     s. 8 222
     s. 9 221
     s. 10 222
     s. 20 232
     s. 23 .... 222, 225
     s. 25 229
     s. 27 224
     s. 27(b) 224
     s. 31 227
     s. 32 227
     s. 37 224
     s. 37(1) 224
     s. 37(2) 224
     s. 37(3) 224
     s. 38(1) 225
     s. 39 225
     s. 40 225

s. 40(5) 226
s. 40(6) 226
s. 44 226
s. 49 234
s. 50(1) 227
s. 50(2) 227
s. 52 7
s. 62 72
s. 69 .... 179, 228
s. 72 ....:. 220, 228
s. 92 228
s. 96 232
s. 97 232
s. 105(6) 72
s. 107 233
s. 108 233
1965 Land Act (No. 2) 142, 161, 182
s. 12 .... 161, 162, 164, 173, 174, 223
s. 45 .... 138, 149, 161, 163, 164, 165, 168, 174, 223
s. 45(1) 164, 165, 168
s. 45(2) 174
s. 45(2)(b) 165
s. 45(3)(a) 167, 168
s. 45(4) 168
s. 45(5) 168
s. 45(6), (7) and (8) 168
s. 45(9)(A) 168
1965 Succession Act (No. 27) . 4, 41, 99, 100, 101, 105, 106, 109
s. 3 112
s. 10(1) 43
s. 11 109
s. 11(1) 13, 43
s. 50(3) 209
s. 56 116
s. 63 .... 108, 109, 116, 117
s. 65 37
s. 66 .... 37, 109, 110
s. 67 .... 37, 109, 110
s. 68 .... 37, 109, 110
s. 69 .... 37, 109, 110
s. 70 .... 37, 109, 110

s. 71 .... 37, 109, 110, 111
s. 71(2) 37, 109
s. 72 .... 37, 109, 111
s. 73 .... 37, 109, 111
s. 74 37
s. 75 37
s. 77 113
s. 78 113
s. 82 .... 116, 117
s. 83 117
s. 85(1) 114
s. 85(2) 114, 115
s. 87 115
s. 94 .... 7, 13
s. 95 12
s. 111 118
s. 112 118
s. 113 .... 118, 119
s. 114 .... 118, 119
s. 115 118
s. 116 118
s. 117 119
1966 Housing Act (No. 21)
s. 114 27
1967 Auctioneers and House Agents Act 119
1967 Landlord and Tenant (Ground Rents) Act (No. 3) 18
s. 30 29
1972 European Communities Act (No. 27) 167
1973 Auctioneers and House Agents Act (No. 23) 199
1976 Family Home Protection Act (No. 28) 173, 243, 245
s. 2 245
s. 3 .... 44, 139, 140, 174, 182
s. 3(1) 246
s. 3(2) 246
s. 3(3) 246
s. 3(4) 246
s. 9 44
s. 12 44
s. 14 241
1980 Finance Act 239

1981 Finance Act (No. 16)
    s. 47 238
1981 Family Law Act 245
    s. 3 247
    s. 4 247
    s. 5 247
    s. 5(1) 248
1982 Finance Act (No. 14) 239
1988 Bankruptcy Act (No. 27) 80
    s. 56 32
1989 Landlord and Tenant (Amendment) Act (No. 2) 18
1992 Irish Land Commission (Dissolution) Act (No. 25) 161
1994 Landlord and Tenant (Amendment) Act (No. 20) 18

Part One

Land Law

Summary of Part One

1. Nature of Real Property   3
2. Freehold Estates   6
3. Leasehold Interests   16
4. Co-Ownership   37
5. Future Interests   45
6. Mortgages   65
7. Easements and Profits   85
8. Succession   99

1

Nature of Real Property

REAL PROPERTY AND PERSONAL PROPERTY CONTRASTED

Real property includes land, mines and minerals, buildings and parts of buildings. It also includes any rights, privileges and benefits derived from land. Personal property may be defined by exclusion, as including all property that is not real property, with the exception of leasehold property.

SPECIAL CLASSIFICATION OF LEASEHOLDS

Lack of seisin by a leaseholder removes leasehold interests from the category of real property. The technical concept of seisin, as it developed historically, became a distinguishing feature of real property. Seisin denotes that a person has: an estate of freehold, in land of freehold tenure and has physical possession of the land or has let the land to a leaseholder or copyholder.

The explanation of leasehold interests falling outside the definition of personal property lies in history. The forms of action framed to protect personal property did not oblige a dispossessor to return the property to its rightful owner – the dispossessor could elect to retain the property and to pay compensation in lieu.

The special form of action developed to protect

leasehold interests, on the other hand, did allow specific recovery to a leaseholder who had been wrongfully dispossessed. "The forms of action," in the words of Maitland, "are buried, but they still rule us from their graves."

DIFFERENCES ARISING FROM THE DISTINCTION BETWEEN REAL AND PERSONAL PROPERTY

First, writing is almost invariably required to transfer an interest in realty. The type of property involved determines whether or not writing is essential on a transfer of personalty.

Secondly, specific recovery in respect of a wrongful dispossession is always available for realty. The general rule, as regards personalty, is to the contrary.

Thirdly, it may be noted that different rules formerly governed the passing of property on death intestate depending on whether the property was real or personal. Devolution of property on death is now however governed by uniform rules contained in the Succession Act, 1965.[1]

TENURE

The concept of tenure imports the idea that one person holds property from another, subject to various conditions and obligations. The concept was critical to the feudal system of landholding – every person holding land under that system held on a particular type of tenure. Tenures were classified into two general categories, i.e., free and unfree. The type of tenure under which land was held dictated the nature of the services and duties owed to the overlord.

---

1. See, infra, Chapter 8 at pages 109-111.

Transfer of land in the early feudal era was possible either by sub-infeudation or by substitution.[2] Resulting from sub-infeudation, the pattern of landholding that evolved under the feudal system was pyramidal. Tenants-in-chief, however, opposed sub-infeudation because it occasioned them a loss of tenurial services. Consequently, they influenced provisions in the Magna Carta, 1217,[3] and in Quia Emptores, 1290.[4] These measures, paradoxically, contributed towards the passing of feudalism.

The Tenures Abolition (Ireland) Act, 1662, abolished most forms of tenure. Therefore, by the late seventeenth century, when English land law had become generally applicable in Ireland, the concept of feudal tenure had been devitalised.

Tenure today still signifies that one person holds land from another. Thus, one may speak of:– (a) freehold tenure, which is a modern derivative of feudal socage tenure, (b) leasehold tenure, which developed independently of the feudal system and (c) tenure, as used in a general sense, to convey that all land is held subject to the ultimate ownership of the State.[5]

---

2. Sub-infeudation involved a process of making sub-grants. Substitution involved a process of replacing one grantee with another.
3. This statute made sub-infeudation difficult by providing that each sub-tenant had to retain sufficient property to enable him to render the feudal services due to his overlord.
4. This, the Statute of Westminster III, 1290, prohibited sub-infeudation.
5. Constitution of Ireland, 1937, Article 10.

2

Freehold Estates

INTRODUCTION

An estate refers to the duration of a person's interest in land. Estates may be either freehold or leasehold. The need for distinguishing between both types of estates derives from the concept of seisin. During the feudal era, the overlord collected feudal services from the person seised of the land, and so it was important to know whether the person on the land had seisin or mere possession. Although the rendition of tenurial services had practically ceased by the end of the seventeenth century – so that the original reason for the importance of seisin no longer existed – nevertheless, the concept of seisin had made a durable impression, not only on the classification of estates, but also on other rules of property law.[1]

Following is an account of the three freehold estates, namely, the fee simple, the fee tail and the life estate.

FEE SIMPLE

A fee simple absolute estate is the nearest one can get to absolute ownership. A fee simple absolute is limited to last forever. It confers the right to use, destroy or alienate

---

1. The importance of seisin in the context of future estates is discussed, infra, in Chapter 5 at pages 53-55.

the land. These rights, however, are restricted by statute and by common law.[2]

A fee simple owner may dispose of his interest by will or by an inter vivos disposition. At common law, a strict rule governs the words of limitation that must be used to convey a fee simple. The property must be conveyed to "T(aker) and his heirs". Any other phrase, such as to "T and his heir", conveys only a life estate. The rule usually applies also on the conveyance of an equitable as well as of a legal fee simple.[3]

The significance of the common law rule regarding words of limitation is diminished by the exceptions to it. These are as follows:

(a) The phrase "in fee simple" may be used instead of "and his heirs".[4]

(b) The rule is inapplicable to a transfer of property that is registered under the Registration of Title Act, 1964.[5]

(c) A gift by will confers the entire interest over which the testator has a power of disposition, even though no words of limitation are used.[6]

(d) A release of his fee simple interest by one joint tenant to another need not contain words of limitation.

(e) A fee simple may be conveyed to a corporation aggregate by the use of the corporate name without words of limitation.

---

2. The Local Government (Planning and Development) Act, 1963, is an instance of restrictions imposed by statute, and the law on nuisance is an instance of restrictions imposed at common law.
3. See, e.g., *Jameson* v. *McGovern* [1934] I.R. 758.
4. Conveyancing Act, 1881, s. 51.
5. Registration of Title Act, 1964, s. 52.
6. Succession Act, 1965, s. 94.

(f) A fee simple may be conveyed to a corporation sole by adding the words "and his successors" to the title of the corporation.

(g) Words of limitation are not necessary to create a fee farm grant under the Renewable Leasehold Conversion Act, 1849.[7]

A fee simple absolute may last forever. Three special forms of fee simple, however, are liable to early determination. These are the determinable fee simple, the fee simple upon condition subsequent and the base fee.[8]

Determinable Fee Simple

This estate lasts only as long as the circumstances described in it continue to exist. The words describing the event that may determine the estate are embodied in the words of limitation. The illustration may be taken of a conveyance "To Bob and his heirs so long as the land is farmed". If Bob or his heirs stop farming the land, the estate ends.

The following words and phrase have been held to indicate a determinable fee: while, during, until, as long as.

If the limitation ceases, the estate naturally ends. Thereupon, the grantor's possibility of reverter, or the appropriate future interest where the possibility of reverter has been disposed of, automatically arises.

Fee Simple upon Condition Subsequent

Like determinable estates, these estates can end when the condition subsequent occurs. The provisions modifying the fee simple are contained in words separate from the words of limitation. The illustration may be taken of a con-

---

7. S. 37.
8. The base fee is discussed, infra, at page 12.

veyance "To Bob and his heirs, but if the land ceases to be used as a farm, then the grantor, his heirs or assigns may re-enter and repossess it". If Bob or his heirs stop farming the land, the estate is liable to be terminated.

The following phrases have been held to indicate a conditional fee: but if, if it happens that, on condition that.

If the condition occurs, the estate does not necessarily terminate. Whether or not it does is at the election of the person with the right of entry.

Determinable and Conditional Fees Distinguished

Since it depends simply on a construction of the words used, and the placings of words in the conveyance, the distinction between these two forms of estates has been described as "little short of disgraceful to our jurisprudence".

Despite its superficial basis, the distinction does however have practical significance. Thus, a condition subsequent, if it occurs, effects the cutting short of a fee simple. The courts have regarded such conditions as more objectionable than determining phrases, since they "interfere with the natural course of an estate". In consequence, conditions subsequent are more liable than determining phrases to be held void on the following bases:

a. that they are imprecise;[9]

b. that they unduly restrict alienation; or

c. that they are illegal, immoral or otherwise contrary to public policy.[10]

Determining phrases, although less likely to be held void on any of the foregoing bases, may nevertheless be

---

9. See, e.g., *Re Coghlan* [1963] I.R. 246.
10. See, e.g., *Re Edgar* [1939] 1 All E.R. 635.

avoided likewise in an appropriate case.[11] It can be noted that the avoidance of a condition subsequent renders the estate in question absolute, whereas the avoidance of a determining phrase results in the failure of the estate in question. This is so since, in the latter event, there will be no proper limitation.

FEE TAIL

By various devices, the landed aristocracy in feudal England sought to keep land within the family through successive generations. The most important technique was the conveyance of land "to T(aker) and the heirs of his body". This form of conveyance, known as the maritagium, had become very popular by 1250. The intent of the settlor would be that the property should follow the words of the limitation, and that no owner should have powers of alienation. The courts, however, took a dim view of such extreme restraints on alienation. Consequently, they interpreted the limitations as "conditional gifts", and conferred a power of alienation on the holder of such an estate on the birth of issue capable of inheriting.

This judicial victory for freedom of alienation was reversed by De Donis Conditionalibus,[12] which was passed after an outcry by settlors concerning the judicial initiatives. The statute provided that "(the) will of the giver. . . shall be from henceforth observed, so that they to whom the land was given under such condition shall have no power to aliene. . .".

The policy of freedom of alienation and various other factors led, in the fifteenth century, to circumvention of De

---

11. See, e.g., *Re Moore* [1888] Ch. D. 116.
12. Statute of Westminster II, 1285.

Donis Conditionalibus. This was done by resort to either fines or recoveries, which were two forms of highly fictitious collusive law actions. In general terms, the effect of either a fine or a recovery was to render the estate freely alienable by the holder.

Fines and recoveries were abolished by the Fines and Recoveries (Ireland) Act, 1834. They were replaced, as methods of barring entails, by the disentailing assurance. The holder of an entail may bar the entail, and so alienate the fee, by executing a disentailing assurance. Such assurance must however be executed with the consent of the "protector of the settlement", an office also created by the 1834 Act. The protector will be either the freeholder in possession of the land or a special protector appointed by the settlor of the entail. Barring the entail under the Act has the effect of enlarging the estate into a fee simple.[13]

Estates tail are either general or special. A general entail arises where property is given to a person, and to the heirs of his body. A special entail arises where the gift is restricted to certain heirs of the grantee's body, and does not go to all of them in general.

General and special entails are further diversified by the distinction of sexes within them, since both may be either in tail male or tail female.

At common law, the words of limitation necessary to convey a general entail inter vivos are "to T(aker) and the heirs of his body/flesh". These words are varied as appropriate where a more restricted type of entail is conveyed, although in all cases the word "heirs" is required.

The alternative phrase "to T(aker) in tail" – modified as appropriate in respect of a more restrictive entail – is now permissible under section 51 of the Conveyancing Act, 1881.

---

13. See, e.g., *Bank of Ireland* v. *Domvile* [1956] I.R. 37.

A gift of a fee tail by will must adhere to the rules for conveying such an estate inter vivos.[14]

After the advent of fines and recoveries, the fee tail lost much of its appeal to settlors as a means of maintaining property within a family. The estate, moreover, has attracted a high incidence of taxation under successive measures. Modern conveyancers use it rarely.

BASE FEE

This estate will arise where a tenant in tail executes a disentailing assurance without having obtained any consent necessary from the protector of the settlement. It will determine on the failure of the heirs of the tenant in tail, unless it has been enlarged in the meantime into a fee simple.

Enlargement may be by:– first, the proper execution of a disentailing assurance; secondly, the purchase by the holder of the fee simple interest; or, thirdly, adverse possession of twelve years after the office of protector becomes vacated.

LIFE ESTATE

Life estates are commonly classified in two broad categories – conventional and legal. Conventional life estates are created by the voluntary action of the owner of land, namely, by deed or will. Legal life estates are created by operation of law.

---

14. Succession Act, 1965, s. 95.

Conventional Life Estates

These arise most commonly as the first estate in a settlement of property. The following illustrates the use of a conventional life estate: Fred, the fee simple owner of a house, wishes to settle the ownership after his death. He may bequeath the house "to my wife for life, remainder in fee simple to Mary my youngest daughter". Another form of conventional life estate is the estate *pour autre vie*. The following illustrates the use of this estate: Tom, the fee simple owner of a house, conveys it "to Joan for the life of Martin, remainder in fee simple to my son John".

Legal Life Estates

These arise from the legal consequences attaching to events concerning other estates. Two illustrations may be taken. First, if there is no longer a possibility that heirs capable of inheriting a fee tail special be born, the entail owner will have merely a life estate. Secondly, a surviving spouse was, until the Succession Act, 1965, entitled to curtesy or dower in the realty of the deceased spouse.[15] Both curtesy and dower conferred life estates only.

Transfer of Life Estates

A life estate may be conveyed inter vivos by direct words of limitation, such as "to T(aker) for life" or "to T(aker) for his wife's life". Also, an abortive attempt to convey another estate may operate to convey an estate for life. For instance, the use of the words "to T(aker) and his heir" with the intention of conveying a fee simple will convey only a life estate. Testamentary dispositions of life estates must accord with the rules necessary to convey a life estate inter vivos.[16]

---

15. See now Succession Act, 1965, s. 11(1).
16. Succession Act, 1965, s. 94.

RIGHTS OF HOLDER OF LIFE ESTATE

Right of Alienation

The general rule is that the holder of a life estate can dispose only of an estate in the land that will not endure longer than his own life estate. By way of exception, if the land is "settled land" within the meaning of the Settled Land Acts, the holder of a life estate may be empowered to dispose of an estate in the land greater than a life estate.[17]

Rights of Enjoyment

The rights of the holder of a life estate to enjoy the property must be circumscribed in order to reconcile them with the rights of the reversioner or remainderman. This topic can be considered under three separate headings, namely, waste, fixtures and emblements.

a. Waste

The reversioner or remainderman may be entitled to prevent the holder of a life estate from committing waste. The law recognises four types of waste, namely, voluntary, ameliorating, permissive and equitable.

Voluntary waste consists of any positive act that alters the character of the land. Examples are opening and working mines on the land, cutting timber and cultivating crops on land used previously for grazing.[18] The holder of a life estate is liable for acts of voluntary waste unless the instrument granting the life estate makes him "unimpeachable for waste".

---

17. See, infra, Chapter 16, pages 205-208.
18. The common law relating to the working of mines and the cutting of timber has been greatly modified by statute.

Ameliorating waste is in all respects similar to voluntary waste – and indeed may be considered simply as a variation of voluntary waste – except that the positive act effecting the change in the character of the property has an improving effect.[19] The courts are unsympathetic to claims for damages or injunctions in respect of this type of waste.

Permissive waste consists of the passive neglect of property.[20] The holder of a life estate may commit permissive waste unless the grant of the estate expressly stipulates to the contrary. In rare instances the grant of a life estate may stipulate that the grantee be "unimpeachable for waste". Such a stipulation effectively gives a licence to commit voluntary waste. Equity qualified the scope of such a licence by introducing the concept of equitable waste. Thus, where the holder of a life estate who is "unimpeachable for waste", commits acts of wanton destruction, he may be made liable for equitable waste.[21].

b. Fixtures

The general rule is that, on its expiry, the holder (or his successors) of a life estate may not remove fixtures. "Fixtures" include anything that has become so attached to property as to form part of the property in law. Trade, ornamental and domestic fixtures are excepted from the general rule.[22]

c. Emblements

The holder or his successor of a life estate has, on its expiry, the right to emblements.[23] This is the right to harvest cultivated crops actually sown by the holder. It is not available where the estate has been determined by the voluntary act of the holder.

---

19. One may take the conversion of a dilapidated building into a habitable residence as an example.
20. A failure to repair buildings could constitute permissive waste.
21. See, e.g., *Vane v. Bernard* [1716] 2 Vern 738.
22. See, e.g., *Shinner v. Harman* [1853] 31 C.L.R. 243.
23. See, e.g., *O'Connell v. O'Callaghan* [1841] Lory & Town 157.

3

Leasehold Interests

INTRODUCTION

The lessee's interest was not, in early feudal times, regarded as an estate. The lessee was recognised as having a personal right over the land. This personal right was protected by a personal action, that gave the lessee a right to damages for interference with his possession, but that did not give the right of specific restitution. This position changed in the late fifteenth century, and it was recognised that a lessee could obtain specific restitution under the writ of ejectione firmae.

Although the lessee, after the fifteenth century, had a fully protected interest in the land, the action by which it was protected was a personal action. His interest therefore continued to be personal property, and so differed considerably from the interests protected by the real actions, which ranked as real property. In modern law, the assimillation of leasehold and freehold interests through statutes and judicial decisions has blurred, but has by no means obliterated, the ancient diversities. It has been aptly stated that:– "The law as to leases is not a matter of logic in vacuo; it is a matter of history that has not forgotten Lord Coke".

The law relating to leases presents one distinctive aspect not common in freeholds, namely, that virtually every leasehold instrument includes numerous promises between lessor and lessee. In some degree, this reflects the parties felt need for complex arrangements concerning matters of importance to them – for example, rent, and modes of securing its payment; the lessee's right to renew the lease, or to purchase the lessor's estate; and restrictions on the lessee's power to use the premises, assign the leasehold, or execute sub-leases. This aspect also reflects the parties' desire to avoid the operation of certain more or less anachronistic rules of law that would regulate their relationship in the absence of manifested agreement.

Leasehold interests had acquired a unique importance in Irish law by the nineteenth century, owing to the earlier social and political history of confiscations and plantations. The prohibitions in the penal laws against freehold estates being given to the native Irish population had resulted in a proliferation of leasehold interests. Moreover, owing to a continuous series of repressive measures, designed to render the native Irish an ownerless class, the Irish tenant had a depressed status in the nineteenth century. The principal grievances concerned insecurity of tenure, unfair rents, lack of freedom of alienation, and lack of legal provision for compensation for improvements or unreasonable disturbance.

Organised agitation on behalf of tenants of pastoral and agricultural holdings led to the Land Purchase Acts, 1870-1923. These Acts addressed the principal grievances, and also conferred rights of compulsory acquisition of the freehold. The ultimate result was that most Irish rural holdings were converted from leasehold to freehold.

RELATIONSHIP OF LANDLORD AND TENANT BASED ON CONTRACT

The affirmation that the relationship of landlord and

tenant is contractual was made in section 3 of Deasy's Act, 1860:[1]

> "The relationship of landlord and tenant shall be deemed to be founded on the express or implied contract of the parties, and not upon tenure or service, and a reversion shall not be necessary to such relation, which shall be deemed to subsist in all cases in which there shall be an agreement by one party to hold land from or under another in consideration for any rent."

Although founded in contract, the landlord and tenant relationship has been subject to much statutory regulation since 1860.[2]

FORMALITIES NECESSARY IN CREATING THE RELATIONSHIP

The Statute of Frauds (Ireland) Act, 1695, in section 2, provides that:

> "No action shall be brought by any person upon any contract of sale of lands unless the agreement upon which such action shall be brought or some memorandum or note thereof shall be in writing and signed by the party to be charged therewith or some other person lawfully authorised to sign."

---

1. Deasy's Act is the common title given to the Landlord and Tenant Law Amendment Act, 1860, (23 & 24 Vict. Cap. 154).
2. Important current legislation includes statutes on ground rents of 1967 and 1978, statutes on private rented dwellings of 1982 and 1983, and statutes of 1971, 1980, 1984, 1989 and 1994 that cover a wide range of issues applicable between landlord and tenant.

That provision, insofar as it applies to the creation of the landlord and tenant relationship, must now be read in the light of section 4 of Deasy's Act, 1860. That section reads:–

> "Every lease or contract with respect to lands whereby the relation of landlord and tenant is intended to be created for any freehold estate or interest, or for any definite period of time not being from year to year or any lesser period, shall be by deed executed, or note in writing signed by the landlord or his agent thereunto lawfully authorised in writing."

In order to appreciate the combined effect of the foregoing provisions, it is necessary to distinguish between two modes whereby the landlord and tenant relationship can be created. First, the relationship may be created by simple contract. In practice, where the relationship is to continue only for a short period, for instance one year, a simple contract only is employed. This contract is usually referred to as "a Letting Agreement". Secondly, the relationship may be created by the use of both a contract and a separate grant of an interest. This mode of creation is normally used when the relationship is to continue for a period longer than one year. It resembles the procedure used on a disposition of freehold.

A leasehold agreement may be enforceable, although it does not comply with the formalities prescribed in the Statute of Frauds and in Deasy's Act. A court may enforce it in favour of a party who has given part performance under the doctrine in *Walsh* v. *Lonsdale*.[3] The operation of that doctrine is dependent on a sufficient act of part performance to enable a court to decree specific performance.

---

3. [1882] 21 Ch. D. 9.

CONTENTS OF THE CONTRACT

It is customary for the parties to a leasehold agreement to expressly set out the incidents of their relationship. The express covenants serve a useful purpose as determinants of the parties' right and liabilities. It is hardly possible, however, even by the most careful negotiation and draftmanship, to eliminate all possibility of dispute. Unforeseen problem situations constantly appear and, even in situations that have been more or less clearly anticipated, litigation may be necessary to resolve conflicts involving the interpretation of covenants.

In general however the major issues of potential dispute can be anticipated, and future conflict can be avoided by appropriate drafting. Thus, it is usual to describe the parties and the property, to specify the term granted, to provide for the amount of rent payable and the manner of its payment, and to allocate responsibility for maintenance, repairs and insurance of the property. Also, the consequences of a default by either party are normally set out.

In addition, special interests of either party can be written into the agreement – for instance, it is common that the landlord impose restrictions in relation to such matters as the use, assignment or sub-letting of the property.

TYPES OF LEASEHOLD INTERESTS

Fixed Terms

A tenancy for a fixed term arises whenever the two parties agree that a tenant will hold the property for a definite period, and no longer. A lease is a classic example; it gives the right to possess the property for six months, or one year, or five years, or ninety-nine years, or for whatever period is agreed. The lease should state with certainty the date of commencement of the term, although secondary evidence may be used to establish this. The date of commencement of the term may pre-date, coincide with, or postdate, the date of the grant of the lease.

The holder of a long term may be entitled to enlarge it into a fee simple under section 65(1) of the Conveyancing Act, 1881.

Renewable Leases and Fee Farm Grants

A renewable lease is one under which the lessee is given a fixed term and also the option to renew. The basic term of a renewable lease may be a term of years, for instance twenty years, or the term may be fixed by reference to lives, for instance for the lives of T(enant) and his wife.

Leases that were perpetually renewable became popular in the eighteenth century. These leases however had two main disadvantages. First, a lessee might forfeit the renewal rights by failure to give timely renewal notice. Secondly, heavy fines were usually payable on renewal. The first disadvantage was removed by section 1 of the Tenantry Act, 1779. This provided that, notwithstanding a lessee's failure to give timely renewal notice, a court may order a renewal if the lessor is compensated for the delay, the lessee has not been guilty of fraud, and the lessee has paid within a reasonable time any fines demanded by the lessor.

A more revolutionary reform of the law governing perpetually renewable leases came about in the Renewable Leasehold Conversion Act, 1849.[4] First, lessees or sublessees of such leases existing in 1849 were given the option of enlarging their interests into fee farm grants. Few availed of this provision, so that the Tenantry Act, 1779, still has

---

4. Renewable Leasehold Conversion Act, 1849, (12 & 13 Vict. c. 105).

relevance in respect of perpetually renewable leases created before 1849. Secondly, the Act provided that perpetually renewable leases could no longer be created after 1849, and that any future grant of such a lease would operate as a fee farm grant. A fee farm grant, arising under the 1849 Act – commonly referred to as a conversion grant – is effectively a statutory fee simple. It is however subject to a fee farm rent, and to any covenants contained in the original lease.

Periodic Tenancies

A periodic tenancy is one that continues indefinitely from one period to another until one party determines it by notice. Such tenancies may be in respect of any period, for instance, weekly, monthly, quarterly, or yearly. They may arise by express grant or by implication. Since a periodic tenancy requires only the payment of a regular rent without any agreement as to a termination date, this estate may arise by virtue of acts of the parties without their ever having expressly agreed to create it.

The period of a periodic tenancy is based upon how the rent is calculated rather than upon how it is paid.

A landlord may elect to treat a tenant who holds over for more than one month after a rightful demand for possession as holding on a yearly tenancy.[5]

Tenancies at Will

This estate arises whenever a landlord permits another person to possess property without any agreement between them as to a termination date or to payment of rent.[6] The tenant's possession will be subject to the under-

---

5. Deasy's Act, 1860, s. 5.
6. See, e.g., *Binions* v. *Evans* [1972] Ch. 359.

standing that either party may determine the tenancy at any time.

Such a tenancy may arise by express grant or by implication. A tenancy at will can arise by implication where, for instance, a purchaser is allowed into possession of land prior to the completion of a sale.

The landlord is entitled to compensation for use and occupation in respect of a tenancy at will that is rent free. This estate is converted into a periodic tenancy, if and when the possessor begins to pay rent, unless the parties show a contrary intention.

Tenancies at Sufferance

A tenant becomes a tenant at sufferance by holding over after the expiration of an agreed term without the prior consent of the landlord.[7] If the landlord permits this, and accepts rent from the tenant, the tenant becomes a periodic tenant. If the landlord requests the tenant to leave, and sues to recover possession, the tenant becomes a trespasser if he remains in possession.[8] But, in the interval between the time when the old tenancy ends and the time when the landlord elects what to do, the tenant is characterised as a tenant at sufferance, viz., a former rightful possessor whose continued possession is justified only by the landlord's inaction.

Tenancies by Estoppel

A landlord is estopped from repudiating a tenancy that he has granted.[9] Consequently, if at the date of the grant the landlord has not sufficient title to support the tenancy,

---

7. See, e.g., *Nixon* v. *Darby* I.R. 2 C.L. 467; and *Caulfield* v. *Farr* I.R. 7 C.L. 469.
8. See, e.g., *Cusack* v. *Farrell*, 18 L.R. Ir. 494.
9. See, e.g., *Gowrie Park Utility Society Ltd.* v. *Fitzgerald* [1963] I.R. 436.

the subsequent acquisition by the landlord of a sufficient title will feed the estoppel, and so regularise the tenant's holding.[10]

RENT

Rent is essential to any contract of tenancy.[11] The persons entitled to rent are the landlord, his heirs or assigns. The persons liable for rent are the tenant, his heirs or assigns.[12]

Rent usually takes a monetary form. Goods, services, or other payments in kind may however constitute rent.

Amount Payable

The amount of rent payable must be fixed by the contract or alternatively must be ascertainable by a method, such as arbitration, prescribed in the contract. The amount payable may be nominal or substantial.

An escalation clause may provide for an increase of rent in certain circumstances. The escalation clause may be designed to take account of inflation, of a breach by the tenant of any covenants or of a change of user of the demised property.

A provision for a specific rent increase on the breach of any covenants by a tenant may represent either a penalty or liquidated damages. If the additional rent is a penalty, it will usually be irrecoverable; also, an ejectment for non-payment of rent will not lie in respect of it.[13]

A tenant who holds over after the expiry of a tenancy

---

10. See, e.g., *Sturgeon* v. *Wingfield* [1846] 15 M. & W. 224.
11. Deasy's Act, 1860, S.3.
12. Deasy's Act, 1860, S.S. 12 and 15.
13. See, e.g., *Annesley* v. *Rooney*, 18 I.L.T.R. 100.

can be made liable for double rent.[14] Rent is considered as accruing from day to day.[15] Consequently, if a leasehold interest terminates prematurely between gale days, an apportionment of the rent due on the termination date must be made.

Rent Payable

Rent is payable on the days, called gale days, specified in the contract. Rent is not payable in advance, unless the contract provides otherwise. Rent is payable notwithstanding the happening of unforeseen events, such as the destruction of the demised property, unless the contract specifies to the contrary. A tenant, however, has a right to surrender his interest on the destruction of the demised property, where the tenant was not at fault.[16] Rent is still payable at common law although the landlord is in breach of a repairing covenant.[17]

Payment of rent before it is due is a valid payment as against a landlord receiving such advance, but is not a valid payment as against a person who receives an assignment of the landlord's interest after the date of the advance payment but before the next gale day.[18]

A receipt for rent paid on a certain gale day is prima facie evidence that the rent for prior gale days has been paid.[19] Although there is no general legal obligation to give a receipt for money, nevertheless, an obligation to give a receipt for rent may be incumbent upon a landlord arising from agreement with the tenant.

---

14. Deasy's Act, 1860, s. 76.
15. Apportionment Act, 1870, s. 2.
16. Deasy's Act, 1860, s. 40.
17. See, e.g., *Corkerry* v. *Stack* 82 I.L.T.R. 60.
18. See, e.g., *Smallman Ltd.* v. *Castle* [1932] I.R. 294.
19. Deasy's Act, 1860, s. 47.

Salvage Payments

A sub-tenant, in order to preserve his interest from forfeiture, may pay the rent owing to the head landlord where the sub-landlord is in default.[20] Such payments are called salvage payments. They are treated as the equivalent, in whole or in part, of the sub-tenant's own rent.

Landlord's Remedies for the Recovery of Rent

A landlord can recover arrears of rent in two principal ways. First, he may sue for the arrears.[21] Secondly, he may levy distress. Distress is a form of self-help remedy: it may be defined as "the taking, without legal process, of goods and chattels on the demised premises as a pledge or security to enforce the payment of rent".

The power of distraining is rarely exercised owing to the many restrictions surrounding it.[22] For instance, entry on the premises for the purpose of distraining must be peaceable, and certain property is protected from distress.

REPAIRS

Liability for repairs as between landlord and tenant may be fixed by contract, or determined under common law or statute. An express contractual term, even of a restricted nature, will exclude an implied covenant on the same matter.[23] For instance, a tenant's covenant to repair the interior of a premises may be taken as excluding any implied liability on the tenant's part under section 42 of Deasy's Act, 1860, to repair the exterior of the premises.

---

20. Deasy's Act, 1860, ss. 20 and 21.
21. Deasy's Act, 1860, s. 45.
22. See, e.g., Ejectment and Distress (Ireland) Act, 1846, ss. 10 and 14; and the Law of Distress Amendment Act, 1908, ss. 1 to 5.
23. See, e.g., *Cowan* v. *Factor* [1948] I.R. 128.

Landlord's Liability

A landlord may be liable for repairs under contract, common law or statute. The extent of a landlord's contractual liability, if any, is determined by interpretation of the repairing covenant.

A landlord is, in general, under no common law liability for repairs. A landlord, however, impliedly covenants that a dwelling will be reasonably fit for occupation in two situations. These are, first, where a furnished dwelling is let for residential occupation and,[24] secondly, where a lessor sells by way of a sub-lease a dwelling that is in the course of construction.[25] Moreover, a landlord may be liable under statute for repairs to certain types of property.[26]

Tenant's Liability

A tenant, in the same way as a landlord, may be liable for repairs under contract, common law or statute.

A tenant impliedly covenants at common law to keep the demised property in reasonable condition. Also, a tenant may be liable at common law for the tort of waste. The common law relating to waste has been modified in its application to landlord and tenant by Deasy's Act.[27]

The principal statutory provision imposing liability for repairs on a tenant is section 42 of Deasy's Act. This provides in part that "every lease shall imply. . . that the tenant shall keep the premises in good and substantial repair and condition". The term "lease" has a special meaning in Irish law. It "shall mean any instrument in writing, whether under seal or not, containing a contract of tenancy in respect

---

24. See, e.g., *Wilson v. Finch Hatton* 2 Ex.D. 336.
25. See, e.g., *Siney v. Corporation of Dublin* [1980] I.R. 400.
26. See, e.g., Housing Act, 1966, s. 114.
27. See, e.g., Deasy's Act, 1860, ss. 25 to 39.

of any lands, in consideration of a rent or return".[28]

Determination of the Extent of Repairing Liability

The extent of a party's repairing liability is determined in accordance with a number of principles, of which the following are the principal ones. First, where there is a repairing covenant, the scope of the covenant must be read in the light of the relevant circumstances. Thus, the initial condition of a premises, its character, age and location, will all be relevant in determining the extent of the liability.[29]

Secondly, a liability for repairs requires neither reconstruction nor decoration.[30] Nevertheless, in a given case, the terms of a repairing covenant may be sufficiently wide to include either reconstruction or decoration.[31] Thirdly, a repairing obligation does not impose liability for "fair wear and tear".[32]

USER OF DEMISED PROPERTY

A tenant's user of demised property may be restricted by express covenant. Such a covenant may, for instance, provide that premises should be used only as a dwelling house.

A tenant's user of demised property is always subject to certain implied covenants as to user. Thus, a tenant is not entitled to adopt a user that is illegal, immoral or tortious.

---

28. Deasy's Act, 1860, s. 1. See, e.g., *Cowan* v. *Factor*, supra at footnote 23.
29. See, e.g., *Fleming* v. *Brennan* [1941] I.R. 499.
30. See, e.g., *Proudfoot* v. *Hart* 25 Q.B.D. 42.
31. See, e.g., *Lurcott* v. *Wakely and Wheeler* [1911] 1 K.B. 905.
32. See, e.g., *Regis Property Co. Ltd.* v. *Dudley* [1949] A.C. 370.

In this connection, it may be noted that a landlord is entitled to determine a lease of a premises where the lessee, tenant or occupier has been convicted of using them as a brothel.[33]

Finally, restrictions on a tenant's user of demised premises may derive from statute such, for instance, as the Local Government (Planning and Development) Act, 1963.

ALTERATIONS TO, AND IMPROVEMENTS OF, DEMISED PROPERTY

A tenant may alter or improve demised property except insofar as prohibited from doing so by express covenant, principles of tort or statute.

INSURANCE OF DEMISED PROPERTY

Covenants requiring the tenant to insure the demised property are common in all leases, although more so in longer leases. Any such covenant is to be construed as requiring the tenant to insure with a recognised company.[34]

ALIENATION OF DEMISED PROPERTY

Alienation of a leasehold interest may occur by operation of law or by voluntary act of the tenant.

Alienation by operation of law occurs:–

a. where a sheriff seizes and disposes of land under a court decree,

---

33. Criminal Law Amendment Act, 1912, s. 5(1).
34. Landlord and Tenant (Ground Rents) Act, 1967, s. 30.

b. on the bankruptcy of a tenant,

c. by a judgement mortgage under the Judgement Mortgage Act, 1850, or

d. on the death of a tenant.

Alienation by voluntary act of the tenant may be either by sub-lease or by assignment. An assignment puts the assignee in privity of estate with the head-lessee. Consequently, where a lease is being alienated on mortgage, it is usual to effect this by sub-lease rather than by assignment.

Any assignment of a leasehold interest, irrespective of its duration, must be by deed or writing.[35]

Leases commonly contain covenants prohibiting alienation. Alienation in breach of such a covenant can make the tenant liable to forfeiture of the leasehold interest, an injunction or damages.

COVENANTS TO YIELD UP POSSESSION

Express covenants requiring a tenant to yield up the property at the determination of the interest are common in leases.

LANDLORD'S OBLIGATIONS TO TENANT

These obligations may be express or implied. Every lease made after 1861 carries the implied covenants – (a) that the landlord shall have title to give the lessee, and (b) that the tenant shall have quiet and peaceable enjoyment

---

35. Deasy's Act, 1860, s. 9.

of the demised property without interruption by any person.[36]

DETERMINATION OF LEASEHOLD INTERESTS

The principal methods of determination of leasehold interests are by:– effluxion of time, notice to quit, surrender, merger or forfeiture. These will be considered in turn.

Effluxion of Time

A tenancy for a fixed term determines on the expiry of the term. Notice to quit is unnecessary in such cases except where a periodic tenancy has arisen by implication at the end of the term.

Notice to Quit

A notice to quit is necessary to determine all periodic tenancies, and also any other tenancy where the contract requires such notice. Notice to quit cannot be in relation only to part of the property. The notice may be given verbally except in relation to agricultural tenancies, in respect of which special written formalities are prescribed by the Notice to Quit Act, 1876.

Either the landlord, the tenant or their respective agents for the purpose may serve the notice. The requisite period of notice may be specified in the contract. If it is not, the requisite period is determined by case law.

Notice to determine a yearly tenancy must be given either: (a) to expire on the last day of the tenancy, or (b) on the last day of the tenancy, to expire six months thence.[37]

---

36. Deasy's Act, 1860, s. 41.
37. See, e.g., *Wright* v. *Tracey* I.R. 8 C.L. 478.

A notice to quit may be served personally or by post. Service at a party's residence will in certain cases suffice. Simply posting a notice on the demised property will constitute a valid service only in certain cases of over-holding. The burden of proving a valid service lies on the party making it. Finally, either party may waive, expressly or impliedly, a notice to quit.[38]

Surrender

A leasehold interest can be surrendered if:– (a) permitted by contract, (b) accepted by the landlord, or (c) permitted under statute.[39]

A surrender of part of a demised property is permissible.[40]

Any surrender must be to the person entitled to the landlord's interest. Such may be, for instance, a mortgagee from the landlord.

In general, the surrender of a head lease involves a surrender of any sub-leases. An exception is where the head- lease is surrendered for purposes of renewal.[41]

Merger

Merger may be described as "(the) annihilation of one estate in another. It takes place usually when a greater estate and a lesser coincide and meet in one and the same person, without any intermediate estate, whereby the lesser is immediately merged – that is, sunk in or drowned – in

---

38. See, e.g., *Curoe* v. *Gordon* 26 I.L.T.R. 95.
39. Surrender under statute is provided for in: Deasy's Act, 1860, s. 40 (on the destruction of the demised premises), the Bankruptcy Act, 1988, s. 56 (on the tenant's bankruptcy), and the Intoxicating Liquor Act, 1927, s. 51 (on the surrender of a licence).
40. Deasy's Act, 1860, s. 44.
41. Deasy's Act, 1860, s. 8.

in the greater". A leasehold interest can determine by merger, as where a tenant becomes entitled to the landlord's interest. The underlying principle is that a person cannot be both landlord and tenant of the same property.

There are three principal restrictions on the doctrine of merger. First, merger will not occur where, although both the landlord's and tenant's interest become vested in one person, some intermediate interest is vested in another person.[42] Secondly, merger will not occur where, although both the landlord's and tenant's interests become vested in the one person, they are not so vested in the same right.[43] Thirdly, no merger will occur unless it is to the benefit of the person in whom both the landlord's and tenant's interests have vested. The latter is an equitable rule.[44]

Forfeiture

Breach by a tenant of a term contained in the contract or le~ ~ may entitle the landlord to damages, an injunction or specific performance. Certain breaches, however, entitle a landlord to exact the penalty of forfeiture of the tenant's interest. A landlord can exact forfeiture where:– (a) the tenant disclaims the landlord's title; (b) the tenant breaches a condition; or (c) the tenant breaches a covenant that is supported by a re-entry clause or a forfeiture clause. At common law, forfeiture of a lease normally effects a termination of all interests derived from it. However, a sub-lessee has a statutory right to apply for relief to the court. The three bases for forfeiture will be now be considered.

---

42. See, e.g., *Mc Ilvenny* v. *Mc Keever* [1931] N.I. 161.
43. The following are illustrations: (1) a tenant's interest vests in the landlord in the latter's capacity as the tenant's personal representative; (2) a tenant's interest vests in a landlord as mortgagee. See, e.g., *Hurley* v. *Hurley* [1908] 1 I.R. 393.
44. See, e.g., *Smith* v. *Chichester* [1848] 12 Ir. Eq. R. 519.

A. Disclaimer of Title

This effects immediate forfeiture. Disclaimer can take a variety of forms. It may consist, for instance, of a purported alienation of the landlord's title by the tenant[45] or of a denial by the tenant of the landlord's interest in an ejectment action,[46] (although the tenant can safely show that the landlord's title has ceased).

B. Breach of Condition

It is necessary that a term be described as a condition in order that it be treated as such. A landlord who asserts that a particular term should be treated as a condition, when it is not so described, bears the burden of proof.

C. Breach of Covenant Supported by Re-Entry Clause or Forfeiture Clause.

Forfeiture will be ordered under this heading only if it is clear that the re-entry or forfeiture clause refers to the covenant alleged to have been broken.

A landlord may waive a tenant's defaults. Such a waiver is binding with respect to a breach of condition, or a breach of covenant supported by a re-entry or forfeiture clause, only if in writing.[47]

Restriction on Forfeiture

The right of forfeiture, except for non-payment of rent or for the breach of certain covenants in mining leases, is restricted by section 14(1) of the Conveyancing Act, 1881. This section provides that a landlord, as a preliminary to exercising forfeiture, must serve a notice on the defaulting

---

45. See, e.g., *Wallace* v. *Daly & Co. Ltd.* [1949] I.R. 352.
46. See, e.g., *O'Reilly* v. *Gleeson* [1975] Unrep. [Sup. Ct., R.I.].
47. Deasy's Act, 1860, s. 43.

tenant. This notice must (a) specify the breach complained of, (b) require the tenant to remedy the breach if it is capable of remedy, and (c) set out any compensation sought by the landlord.

The landlord can proceed to forfeiture only if the demands contained in the notice are not met by the tenant within a reasonable time.

Reliefs against Forfeiture

Two reliefs against forfeiture are contained in the Conveyancing Acts of 1881 and 1892. First, a tenant may apply to the court for relief in respect of any forfeiture to which section 14(1) of the Conveyancing Act 1881 applies.[48] The court's power of granting relief is discretionary and will be exercised having regard to the conduct of the parties and all other relevant circumstances.[49]

Secondly, a sub-lessee may apply to the court for relief where the intermediate lessor's interest has become liable to forfeiture.[50] The court may vest the intermediate lessor's interest in the sub-lessee except that any interest so vested may not exceed the term of the sub-lessee's original interest. Relief may be granted on such conditions as the court thinks reasonable.

Statutory Ejectment

In addition to exacting forfeiture of a tenant's interest in accordance with the rules previously set out, a landlord may be entitled to eject a tenant on a statutory basis. For instance, a landlord is entitled to the ejectment of a tenant whose rent is in arrears for one year, and whose tenancy

---

48. Conveyancing Act, 1881, s. 14(2).
49. See, e.g., *Breaden* v. *Fuller & Son Ltd.* [1949] I.R. 290.
50. Conveyancing Act, 1892, s. 4.

is greater than from year to year.[51]

A tenant may seek relief from the court in an action for statutory ejectment for non-payment of rent. Even after an ejectment order has been executed, the tenant may yet redeem the lost tenancy through an application to the court for relief made within six months of the execution. The redemption will be allowed if the tenant tenders the arrears.[52]

---

51. Deasy's Act, 1860, s. 52.
52. See also, e.g., statutory ejectment for overholding Deasy's Act, 1860, s. 72; and statutory ejectment for desertion, Deasy's Act, 1860, s. 78.

4

Co-ownership

INTRODUCTION

The term co-ownership is sometimes used to refer to any situation in which two or more persons simultaneously may assert interests referable to an item of realty. As instances, one may refer to the relationships of lessor and lessee, mortgagor and mortgagee, and life tenant and remainderman. In the narrower sense in which lawyers use the term, "co- ownership" refers only to situations in which two or more persons simultaneously have rights to the possession of property. Such a situation may be created in various ways. For instance, an owner may die intestate, survived by two or more persons who succeed to ownership as tenants in common.[1] Another instance arises where two or more persons purchase the same realty, as where a husband and wife purchase a house. A third instance is where the ownership of land is acquired by two or more persons through adverse possession.

Irish law recognises only a limited number of forms of co-ownership. The basic ones now in use are joint tenancy and tenancy in common. Another recognised form – that however arises only rarely at the present time – is coparcenary. Tenancy by entireties was an earlier form of co-ownership that arose when property was conveyed to husband and wife as joint tenants, but it is obsolete today.

---

1. Succession Act, 1965, ss. 65 to 75.

JOINT TENANCY AND TENANCY IN COMMON

General

Joint tenancy is rooted in the concept that the co-owners comprise, for at least one purpose, not a number of individuals, each owning an undivided interest, but a corporate entity – a singular legal entity that owns the property.[2] Tenancy in common, by contrast, is based on the concept of undivided interests. Tenants in common are conceived as owning fractional interests that may be equal or unequal.[3]

CHARACTERISTICS

There is one distinguishing feature of a tenancy in common, namely, unity of possession. In a joint tenancy there are three additional unities, i.e., unities of interest, of title and of time.

Unity of Possession

This means that each co-owner has a right to possess the entire property. It is the only unity essential to a tenancy in common.

Unity of Interest

This means that the co-owners have like interests in the property. The nature of the interest, i.e., freehold or leasehold, must be the same. Also, the extent and duration of the interests must be the same. Unity of interest must apply to the estate that is held jointly; but if that require-

---

2. See, e.g., *Cockerill* v. *Gilliland* [1854] 6 Ir. Jur [O.S.] 357.
3. *Cockerill* v. *Gilliland, ibid.*

ment is satisfied, it does not matter that one joint tenant has a further and separate interest in the same property.

Unity of Title

This means that the interests of the co-owners derive from the same act (for instance, adverse possession) or instrument (for instance, a will or a conveyance).

Unity of Time

This means that the interests of the co-owners must vest at the same time. Unity of time is not essential to a joint tenancy in two cases, i.e., where co-owners acquire their interests either by a conveyance to uses, or by a testamentary disposition.

PREFERENCES FOR ONE FORM OF CO-OWNERSHIP OVER ANOTHER

A rule of construction favouring joint tenancy was developed at common law.[4] Consequently, unless a transferor clearly manifests an intent to create a tenancy in common, a joint tenancy will be presumed. This rule is ascribed to a feudal policy opposed to the division of ownership. Such division, it will be seen, is less likely under joint tenancy, since this form of co-ownership carries the right of survivorship.

Even at common law, the inference of joint tenancy may be reversed if the dispositive instrument contains words of severance, i.e., expressions indicating that the transferees are to take separate shares in the property. An instance would be a conveyance of property in fee simple

---

4. See, e.g., *McDonnell* v. *Jebb* [1865] 16 Ir. Ch.R. 359.

in equal shares, share and share alike, equally or respectively. Such words of severance create a tenancy in common as distinct from a joint tenancy.[5]

Although generally in accord with the common law, equity leans against joint tenancy.[6] The chancery courts favoured tenancy in common, because it frequently achieves a fairer division of property than does joint tenancy. These courts could not overrule the common law inference. They could however oblige co-owners, who held as joint tenants at common law, to hold the property on trust for themselves as tenants in common in equity. Equitable innovation is now practically arrested in this area, and the equitable preference for tenancy in common is largely confined to the following situations:– first, where co-owners have contributed unequally to the purchase price of property;[7] secondly, where co-owners have acquired property as security for loans made by them;[8] and thirdly, where partners hold property of the firm as co-owners.[9]

CONSEQUENCES OF DIFFERENT TYPES OF CO-OWNERSHIP

Survivorship (Jus Accrescendi)

The chief and special aspect of joint tenancy is that of survivorship:– upon the death of one of the co-owners, the surviving co-owner becomes the sole owner of the entire

---

5. See, e.g., *Re Robson* [1940] Ir. Jur. Rep. 72 – the word "shares" was held to give rise to a tenancy in common. See also, e.g., *Kennedy* v. *Ryan* [1938] I.R. 620.
6. See, e.g., *Fleming* v. *Fleming* [1855] 5 I.R. Ch.R. 129.
7. See, e g., *O'Connell* v. *Harrison* [1927] I.R. 330.
8. See, e.g., *Petty* v. *Styward* [1632] 2 Ch. Rep. 57.
9. See, e.g., Hawkins v. Rogers [1951] I.R. 48.

estate.[10] During the lives of both joint tenants, each is viewed as owning the entire estate, subject only to the equal claims of the other. Upon the death of one of them, the other's already full ownership is merely freed from the one disability previously existing, i.e., the equal claim of the deceased.

Tenancy in common does not carry the right of survivorship. Tenants in common have separate, but still undivided, interests in property. Consequently, the interest of a deceased tenant in common will devolve according to the terms of his will or, where there is no will, according to the rules governing intestate succession that are set out in the Succession Act, 1965.[11]

Severance

A joint tenancy may be severed, thereby converting it into a tenancy in common.

A joint tenant may sever the joint tenancy by conveying, in whole or in part, his interest to any other person.[12] Similarly, a judgement creditor of a joint tenant, by writ of execution, can force a sale of the debtor's undivided interest, and the forced sale will effect a severance, just as a voluntary conveyance will do. Again, severance may be effected if one joint tenant acquires a further interest in the property subsequent to the creation of the joint tenancy.[13] Finally, severance will occur in equity even where a joint tenant merely contracts to alienate his interest.[14]

It can be noted that each of the severance methods above involves the elimination of the unities of time and

---

10. See, e.g., *Cockerill* v. *Gilliland*, supra at footnote 2. The principle is the same where there are more than two co-owners.
11. See, infra, Chapter 8 at pages 109-111.
12. See, e.g., *Connolly* v. *Connolly* [1866] 17 I.R. Ch.R. 208.
13. See, e.g., *Flynn* v. *Flynn* [1930] I.R. 337.
14. See, e.g., *Frewen* v. *Relfe* [1787] 2 Bro. C.C. 220.

title that would previously have existed. Also, it bears emphasis that a joint tenancy may not be severed by will.

The new co-owner after a severance holds an undivided interest in the property and co-ownership remains. The new co-owner, relative to the existing co-owner(s), is a tenant in common. The severance of one joint tenant's interest will not however affect the relationship of two or more others – they will be treated as continuing to hold their interests in joint tenancy.

Partition

Co-ownership will be satisfactory so long as the co-owners are in harmony concerning the use to be made of their common resource – the sharing of any revenue it may yield, the allocation of the costs of ownership such as taxes, maintenance and insurance and perhaps other matters. If, however, harmony is lacking, the most attractive alternative may be to effect termination of the co-ownership by partition.

A partition is a physical division of the property. It converts the former co-owners into neighbours. It differs from severance in that severance does not alter co-ownership, but merely eliminates the element of survivorship.

The physical division of property by partition may occur either by agreement, or by court action. The co-owners may agree on the partition and may convey cross deeds effecting it.[15] Alternatively, the court may compel partition in an action brought by one of the co-owners under the Partition Acts.[16] In some circumstances, the physical partition of property may not make sense.[17] In such instances,

---

15. Real Property Act, 1845, s. 3.
16. Partition Acts, 1868 and 1876.
17. See, e.g., *Turner* v. *Morgan* [1803] 8 Ver. 143, a case that involved the partition of a house into thirds.

the court may order a sale instead of partition, and may order the division of the proceeds between the co-owners.[18]

Determination of Co-ownership by Union

A joint tenancy may be determined by severance. Partition will determine either joint tenancy or tenancy in common. Both of these forms of co-ownership may also be determined by union of the interests in a sole tenant, i.e., where the entirety of the property becomes vested in a single owner.

COPARCENARY

This form of co-ownership arises where property descends to two or more persons who, together, constitute the "heir". Its incidence is extremely rare in present law, since the Succession Act, 1965, abolished the common law rules for the ascertainment of the heir. These rules are retained only regarding the descent of unbarred entails.[19]

Coparcenary combines elements of both joint tenancy and tenancy in common. Thus, the four unities are normally present. On the other hand, coparceners hold in undivided shares and no right of survivorship applies between them.

TENANCY BY ENTIRETIES

This form of co-ownership was connected from the outset with the concept adopted in law, because of religious doctrine, that husband and wife were one flesh, one personality. It arose where property was conveyed to

---

18. See, e.g., *Re Hawkesworth's Estate* [1878] 1 L.R. I.R. 179.
19. Succession Act, 1965, ss. 10(1) and 11(1).

husband and wife as joint tenants – they took the property as tenants by entireties. In effect, this meant that the husband acquired beneficial ownership of the property.

The right of a wife to hold property in her own right was established in the Married Women's Property Act, 1882. This statute marked the last of the days, at least in property law, when "husband and wife were one, and the husband was the one". A conveyance of property to husband and wife as joint tenants creates, since 1882,[20] a joint tenancy. Tenancy by entireties is obsolete.

FAMILY HOME PROTECTION ACT, 1976

This Act does not render husband and wife co-owners of the family home. Its principal purpose is to give each spouse an interest in the family home and thus to restrict the power of the other spouse to dispose of it unilaterally. This is achieved by section 3, which provides that a purported conveyance by a spouse of any interest in the family home to any person except the other spouse, without the prior consent of the other spouse, is void.

The Act contains other provisions relating to the disposal of chattels from the family home.[21] It provides also for the registration of notices of the existence of a marriage in the Land Registry and the Registry of Deeds.[22] Finally, it provides for exemption from certain duties and fees where property is being transferred from the name of one spouse into the joint names of the spouses,[23] thus facilitating the creation of co-ownership between spouses in the family home.

20. Married Women's Property Act, 1882, ss. 1 and 5.
21. Family Home Protection Act, 1976, s. 9.
22. Ibid., s. 12.
23. Ibid., s. 14.

5

Future Interests

INTRODUCTION

Every interest in land is either present or future. A present interest entitles its owner to an immediate right to the land. A future interest is an estate that will or may become possessory at some future time subsequent to its creation. The owner of a future interest has to await the termination of preceeding estates before entering into possession. The future interest may of course be of great value prior to that time. It is inheritable and may usually be conveyed by deed or will. Also, as has been seen,[1] an owner of a future interest may be protected against waste by the owner of a present estate.

Future interests arise most commonly in the context of property settlements. A settlement of property is made when a person wishes to divide the ownership of property so that different persons will take successive estates in it.

The rules governing future interests are, in general, restrictive of settlors. They advance various policies that have, over the centuries, become part of the rubric of real property law. Thus, for instance, many of the rules were created by judges in an attempt to make land alienable and, thereby, to defeat the efforts of landowners to exert dead-hand control through successive generations.

A lawyer may be called on to apply a knowledge of

---

1. See, supra, Chapter 2 at pages 14 and 15.

future interest rules, first, as an estate planner. It has been aptly stated in this context that "Practically anything a testator is likely to want can be done. . . Wills fail because of the inept work of lawyers, not because of excessive demands of the testator". A knowledge of future interest rules may be invoked, secondly, in opposing a settlement. The opponent, in a typical situation, will stand to gain by the setting aside of the settlement.

VESTED AND CONTINGENT INTERESTS

The distinction between vested and contingent interests is crucial to many of the future interest rules and, so, must be considered at the outset. An estate is vested in possession where the person entitled to it has a right to present possession. For instance, a grant "to (T)aker for life" will give the transferee the right to present possession.

An estate is vested in interest if:– first, the person or persons entitled to it are ascertained, and, secondly, such a person or persons have a present unqualified right to take possession of the estate subject only to the determination of any prior interests.[2] One may instance a grant "to John for life, remainder in fee simple to Mary":– Mary has an estate that is vested in interest.

An estate that is neither vested in possession nor in interest is said to be contingent. Alternatively, an estate is contingent if some event, other than the determination of prior interests, is necessary before the person entitled to it will have an unqualified right to the estate.[3] The following is an illustration:– a grant "to Helen for life, remainder to Bob for life, remainder in fee simple to Donal as soon as he

---

2. See, e.g., *Martin* v. *Mc Causland* [1842] 4 Ir. L.R. 340.
3. See, e.g., *Re Mansfield* [1962] I.R. 454.

reaches 21", where Donal has not reached 21 at the date of the grant. Donal's estate will be contingent until he reaches 21.

TYPES OF FUTURE INTERESTS

Reversions

When a grantor conveys a present estate smaller than the one he owns, the residue is a future interest. Usually this is a reversion. If Tom, the owner of a fee simple absolute conveys a term for years, a life estate or a fee tail to Joan, Tom retains a reversion in fee simple. All reversions are vested in interest.

Future interests in the grantor that are not reversions – possibilities of reverter and rights of entry – have already been referred to.[4]

Remainders

When a grantor conveys an estate smaller than the one he owns and, in the same instrument, conveys a further estate to commence after the first estate, the latter estate is a remainder.

A remainder may be either vested or contingent. It is vested if it is ready to take effect on the termination of the particular or immediate estate(s). It is contingent if it is subject to a contingency other than the termination of the particular estate before it can take effect. The distinction between vested and contingent remainders may be explained in the following terms:– "The chief characteristic which distinguishes a vested from a contingent remainder is the present capacity to take effect in possession should the possession become vacant, with the certainty that the

---

4. See, supra, Chapter 2 at pages 8 and 9.

event upon which the vacancy depends will sometime happen. . . . In the case of a vested remainder, there is a person in being ascertained and ready to take, who has a present right of future enjoyment which is not dependent upon any uncertain event or contingency while, in a case of a contingent remainder, the right itself is uncertain."[5]

Both vested and contingent remainders must comply – and may be avoided if they do not comply – with certain common law rules deriving from the seisin concept. These rules will be seen later. Contingent remainders, it will be noticed, are especially vulnerable. Executory interests, the final type of future interests, are largely unaffected by the seisin-derived rules.

Executory Interests

The development of executory interests is a somewhat involved one. Its beginning is in "the ancient practice of men putting their trusted friends in possession of their lands, in confidence that their friends would dispose thereof according to their wishes", i.e., the practice of conveying to uses. The following is an example of a type of conveyance to uses that was common in the fourteenth century:– a conveyance by Bob "to Carl and his heirs to the use of myself, Bob, and my heirs". The reasons why an owner in feudal times would put another into legal possession included the following:– to defraud creditors, to avoid feudal services or to provide for the devolution of property on his death.[6]

The common law courts did not recognise the interest of the cestui que use, i.e., the person for whose benefit the legal owner held his title. At common law, therefore,

---

5. The distinction is elaborated on in *Re Mansfield* [1962] I.R. 454.
6. Powers of testation were not fully recognised until 1540.

neither the feoffer (the transferor) nor the cestui que use could enforce the use against the feoffee to uses (the person entrusted with the legal ownership). The chancery courts did, however, recognise the interest of the cestui que use and would enforce it against the feoffee to uses. The reason for the difference of approach between the common law and chancery courts was that, at that time, the chancery courts were courts of conscience:– "Men ought to fulfill their promises, their agreement. The feoffee to uses must comply with the use because he has agreed to do so."

A combination of circumstances, particularly Henry VIII's need to revive, as a source of revenue, the incidents of feudal tenure that had been much evaded by the separation of legal and equitable ownership, brought about a massive attack on uses in the sixteenth century. Henry found powerful allies in the judges of the common law courts and the lawyers who practised before them – these were unwilling to see chancery and its bar dominant in matters of land.

The attack came in the Statute of Uses, 1536,[7] which, according to Maitland, was "forced upon an extremely unwilling Parliament by an extremely strongwilled King". The statute sought to prevent the splitting of ownership by providing that the "beneficial" owner of land should be considered the legal owner. In the terminology adopted, the use was executed and thus transformed into a legal interest.

Inevitably, attempts to evade the statute quickly followed its enactment. The evasion device that was eventually to succeed met initial failure when it came before the common law courts in Tyrrel's Case, 1557:[8]

Jane Tyrrel conveyed her lands to her son, G. Tyrrel,

---

7. The statute was adopted in Ireland by the Statute of Uses (Ireland) 1634.
8. [1557] 2 Dyer 155a.

to the use of the said G. Tyrrel and his heirs to the use of the said Jane during her life, ... Jane had no doubt been advised that, although the first use would be executed by the statute, the second use and the interests created by it would take effect as before the statute. The court however demurred with the words "an use cannot be engendered of an use".

After Tyrrel's Case, the rule was settled, so far as the common law courts were concerned, that "a use upon a use" was void. Chancery courts also adhered to this rule for a century after the statute was enacted. With the lapse of time, however, great social and economic changes occurred that rendered the policy of the statute obsolete and that obviated serious objections to the separation of legal and equitable ownership. In particular, other forms of taxation had rendered feudal incidents relatively unimportant as a source of revenue. In consequence, chancery courts again commenced to prevent a legal owner from violating an agreement or understanding that another or others should have beneficial ownership. In other words, Chancery began to recognise the second use.[9]

Chancery's recognition of the second use has had a major influence on property law. It led to the development of the modern trust, and also made possible the creation of new forms of future interests. These developments will now be reviewed.

(i) Splitting of Ownership Again Possible, and Development of the Trust.

It again became possible to split ownership into legal and equitable components by employing a use upon a use. The older form of conveyancing was:– "to James in fee simple

---

9. See, e.g., *Sambach* v. *Dalston* [1634] Tothill 168.

to the use of John in fee simple to the use of Joseph in fee simple." John became the legal owner by reason of the operation of the Statute of Uses, and Joseph became the beneficial or equitable owner because of Chancery's recognition of the second use.

The terminology has now altered and a form of legal shorthand is adopted. The modern form of conveyance is:– "unto and to the use of John in fee simple in trust for Joseph in fee simple." John becomes legal owner and Joseph becomes equitable owner. In the words of one commentator, John has "the skin of the orange" and Joseph has "the juice".

Chancery's recognition of the second use was, therefore, the genesis of the modern trust. The reasons for creating trusts today differ from the reasons that gave rise to the creation of uses in feudal times. One important purpose today is to provide estate management and to relieve the beneficial owner of this burden. Trustees today frequently have many active duties.

(ii) New Forms of Future Interests, namely, Executory Interests, Became Possible.

Common law seisin rules, that are considered later, restrict the variety of future interests that are possible where the trust concept is not used. Thus, at common law, it is possible neither to have a springing remainder, nor a shifting remainder. Also, contingent remainders that do not vest in time are void.[10]

Earlier decisions decreed that the new forms of executory interests made possible by the employment of a second use were likewise restricted by the common law seisin-derivative rules. These decisions however were overruled

---

10. See infra at pages 53-55.

in the early seventeenth century and, as has been graphic-
ally remarked, "went down with the judges who made
them like chopped hay". As a result, executory interests,
whether created by deed or will, can be either springing or
shifting.

One may consider the following illustrations of executory interests created by deed:–

> (1) Springing use; grant "unto and to the use of Liam
> in fee simple in trust for Michael when he reaches 21."
> The use here, when it is executed (sprung), does not
> interfere with a previously executed use.
>
> (2) Shifting use; grant "to Donal in fee simple to the
> use of Charles in fee simple until Frank marries and
> then to the use of Frank in fee simple". The use here
> in favour of Frank, when it is executed (shifted), inter-
> feres with the previously executed use in favour of
> Charles.

These illustrations demonstrate another distinction
possible in inter vivos executory interests. Thus, the first
is of an equitable springing use. The second is of a legal
shifting use.

Executory interests created by will are referred to as
executory devises. They share with executory interests
created inter vivos the element of a splitting of ownership
and the element of futurity, i.e., the executory devise will
not be enjoyed until some time after the testator's death.
Executory devises, however, will be given effect even
though they are not framed in terms of uses or trusts. So
long as a will is clear on the futurity aspect, an executory
devise will operate as a springing devise or as a shifting
devise, as the case may be.[11] The following is an illustration

---

11. See, e.g., *Taylor* v. *Bydall* [1677] 1 Freem. K.B. 24; and *Fulmerston* v.
    Steward [1596] Cro. Jac. 592.

of a springing devise not employing "use terminology":–
devise "to Linda in fee simple until Tracy marries, and then
to Tracy in fee simple."

RULES GOVERNING THE VALIDITY
OF LEGAL REMAINDERS

Chancery's recognition of executory interests made
possible an entirely new range of future interests. This
becomes clear only by examination of the rules restrictive
of future interests at common law. These rules, that still
apply to future interests not employing the use or trust
(except to executory devises), were developed by the judges
in feudal times. The rules, when developed, promoted a
variety of policies:– they hindered dead-hand control; they
precluded an abeyance of seisin; and they permitted estates
"to run their natural course".

The following is an account of the rules.

Rule 1

A contingent remainder of freehold, unless it is
supported by a particular freehold estate, is void. Stated
alternatively, springing remainders are void. The following
is an illustration:– a grant "to Bernard for life from May 1
next". Bernard's interest is void.

Rule 2

A remainder after a fee simple is void. The following
is an illustration:– a grant "to Angela in fee simple, remainder to Marie in fee simple". Marie's interest is void.

Rule 3

A remainder to take effect in possession by cutting
short a particular (intermediate) estate is void. Stated alternatively, shifting remainders are void.

Rule 4

A remainder that does not, in fact, vest in interest during the continuance of a particular estate, or at the moment of its determination, is void.

The special liability to destruction of contingent remainders derives from this rule. Two sets of circumstances are distinguishable. First, it may be clear at the date of a settlement that a contingent remainder will not vest in interest in time; for instance, a grant "to Michael for life and one day after his death to Philip in fee simple". Philip's interest is invalid from the outset. Secondly, it may be unclear at the date of a settlement whether a contingent remainder will vest in time; for instance, a grant "to Paul for life, remainder to Owen in fee simple when he reaches 21" where Owen is under 21 at the date of the settlement. Here, the "wait and see" rule applies. One does not designate Owen's interest as invalid from the outset. One waits to see whether, in fact, Owen becomes 21 before Paul dies – if he does his interest is valid; otherwise, it is void.

The Contingent Remainders Act, 1877,[12] has moderated Rule 4. Since that Act, a contingent remainder must first be tested by reference to the rule to ascertain if it is valid at common law. If the remainder does not vest in time, one can then assume that the future interest had been given instead by way of executory interest. This statutory permissible mode of construction insulates the contingent remainder from failure under rule 4 above. A future interest might still however be invalidated under one of the perpetuity rules to be considered later.

It may be noted that remainders were also formerly liable to artificial destruction by disseisin with loss of the right of entry, forfeiture, surrender, merger or disclaimer. These methods of destruction were abolished by the Real

---

12. Contingent Remainders Act, 1877 (40 and 41 Vict. c. 33).

Property Limitation Act, 1833,[13] the Real Property Act, 1845,[14] and the Contingent Remainders Act, 1877.

A summary of the position relating to the common law seisin rules may now be given. Future interests created at common law are liable to invalidation under the seisin-derivative rules, although the pitfalls of rule 4 have been negated by statute. Future interests created by way of executory interests are unfettered by these rules.[15] Consequently, executory interests permit a greater flexibility to settlors in providing for the disposition of property in the future. It is rare therefore for conveyancers, except in the case of the simplest types of settlements, not to employ executory interests in preference to future interests created at common law.

RULES GOVERNING THE REMOTENESS OF VESTING OF FUTURE INTERESTS

The development of unfettered executory interests raised a new spectre for the courts, namely, the settlement that could dictate ownership into perpetuity. New restrictive rules were necessary. These rules, while they would need to recognise the legitimate desire of owners to settle the future ownership of their property, would need also to implement the policy that property not be rendered inalienable.

The more important of these rules will now be considered.

---

13. Real Property Limitation Act, 1833, ss. 4, 5 and 39.
14. Real Property Act, 1845, s. 8.
15. Executory interests had to comply with rule 4 during one period under the decision in *Purefoy* v. *Rogers*, 1671. That case was overruled by the Contingent Remainders Act, 1877.

RULE IN *WHITBY* V. *MITCHELL*[16]

The rule may be stated as follows:– "If an interest in realty is given to an unborn person, any remainder to his issue is void, together with all subsequent limitations."

The following points deserve notice. First, the rule applies only to remainders, and not to executory interests. Secondly, the rule has no wait and see element. Thirdly, even a vested remainder may fail under the rule.

Application of the rule to testamentary settlements may be mitigated by the cy près doctrine. Limitations, that might otherwise fail under the rule, may be construed as gifts in tail to the first unborn beneficiary.[17] This qualification, confined to testamentary settlements, derived from the judicial recognition that many wills are made without professional advice.

The shortcomings of the rule under discussion are manifest. By reason of its confinement to when successive remainders are given to unborn persons, and of its inapplicability to executory interests, the catching scope of the rule is too narrow to meet the problem of perpetuities. Moreover, since a future interest may be valid under the modern rule against perpetuities, but invalid under *Whitby* v. *Mitchell*, the latter rule may be regarded as a trap for the unwary draftsman.

THE RULE AGAINST PERPETUITIES

A working formulation of the rule is as follows:– "No interest is good unless it must vest, if at all, not later than twenty one years after some life in being at the creation of

---

16. [1890] 44 Ch.D. 85.
17. See, e.g., *Parfitt* v. *Hember* [1867] L.R. 4 Eq. 443.

the interest." The above formulation proves adequate in the majority of cases that arise. A more comprehensive formulation however is as follows:–

> "Every attempted disposition of a future interest in land to a person or persons is void unless, at the time when the instrument creating it takes effect, one can say that the future interest must vest (if it vests at all) within à life or lives then in being and twenty one years after the termination of such life or lives, with the possible addition of periods of gestation. If there is no relevant life, then only twenty one years is allowed as the perpetuity period."

The rule invalidates interests that vest too remotely. It is not a rule invalidating interests that last too long. The various elements of the rule will be considered in turn.

Perpetuity Period

This is based on the maximum period for which property may be tied under an entail settlement. The circumstances in which the holder of an entail may bar the entail, thus converting the estate into a fee simple, have already beer referred to. The effect of a disentailing assurance is to free the property from the entail settlement and to enlarge the estate into a fee simple.[18]

Required Certainty of Vesting

Looking forward from when the dispositive instrument takes effect, it must be certain (not merely probable) that a future interest will vest in interest within the perpetuity period. Otherwise it is invalid. Many perfectly

---

18. See, e.g., *Re Kelly* [1932] I.R. 255.

reasonable dispositions are struck down on some outside chance of a too remote vesting. Consider, first, the "fertile octogenarian" type of case.

> Testator has a widowed sister, Gail, aged 80. He leaves property in trust "to pay the income to Gail for life, then to pay the income to the children of Gail for their lives, then to pay the principal to the children of such children". The gift of the principal is bad under the traditional English view; for the children of Gail include after-born children, and Gail is conclusively presumed to be capable of having children until death.

A different view of this type of case prevails in Ireland.[19]

The "unborn widow" type of case furnishes another colourful illustration.

> Testatrix has a son, Henry, 45 years old. The son has a wife and grown children. Testatrix leaves property in trust "to pay the income to Henry for his life, then to pay the income to Henry's widow, if any, for her life, and then to pay the principal to the children of Henry then living." The gift of the principal is invalid. Henry may marry again, and his second wife may be a person who was unborn at the death of the testatrix.

Vesting in Interest

A remainder complies with the rule as soon as it becomes vested, regardless of when it becomes possessory. The following is an illustration:– a devise "to Brian for life, remainder to Brian's children for their lives, remainder to Edward (an identified person) in fee simple". Edward's interest is good; it is presently vested, though clearly it may

---

19. See, e.g., *Exham* v. *Beamish* [1939] I.R. 336.

not come into possession until the death of a child of Brian yet unborn – a point well beyond the period of perpetuities.

Application of the Rule to Gifts to Classes

The perpetuity rule applies with particular stringency to class gifts; if a single member of the class might possibly take a vested interest outside the period, the entire gift fails.[20] For instance, the whole gift to the children in the following illustration is invalid under the rule. A testator bequeaths a fund "in trust for Martin for life, and then in trust for Martin's children who shall reach the age of 25", where four children of Martin are living at the date of death.

Two important limitations on the class-gift rule must be mentioned. First is the rule that, where there is a gift of a specific sum to each person described by a class designation, some members may take their gifts, though the gifts to others are void.[21] Second is the rule of construction whereby the class closes when the interest of the first member becomes vested.[22]

Powers of Appointment and the Rule against Perpetuities

The distinction between general and specific powers must first be made. A general power is one that permits appointment to anyone, including the donee of the power – for instance, a devise "to Eleanor for life, and then to such person or persons as Eleanor shall appoint". A special power is one that permits appointment only to a designated class – for instance, a devise "to Eleanor for life, and then to such of Eleanor's children as Eleanor shall appoint".

With reference to the rule against perpetuities, two issues arise:-- first, is the power valid?; and secondly, assum-

---

20. See, e.g., *Re Taylor's Trusts* [1912] 1 I.R. 1.
21. See, e.g., *Re Ewart's Estate* [1967] 18 N.I.L.Q. 463.
22. See, e.g., *Re Poe* [1942] I.R. 535.

ing the power to be valid, is the interest that has been appointed in the exercise of the power valid?

Validity of the Power

A special power is void if it is capable of being exercised beyond the period of perpetuities.[23] A general testamentary power stands on the same footing as a special power. A general power exercisable by deed or will is the equivalent of ownership; it is valid if it must be acquired by the donee within the period of perpetuities.

Validity of Appointed Interests

When an appointment is made under a special power, the appointment is read back into the instrument creating the power, as if the donee were filling in blanks in the donor's instrument, and the period of perpetuities is computed from the date the power was created. However, facts and circumstances existing at the date the appointment is made are considered in determining the validity of the appointment – there is a wait and see element.[24] When an appointment is made under a general testamentary power, the same rules apply: the validity of the appointment is determined by computing the period of perpetuities from the date of creation of the power.

When an appointment is made under a general power, exercisable by deed or will, the validity of the appointment is determined by computing the period of perpetuities from the date of the appointment.

---

23. See, e.g., *Re De Sommery* [1912] 2 Ch. 622. There is however authority for the proposition that a "wait and see" element is permissible. See, e.g., Re Witty [1913] 2 Ch. 666.
24. See, e.g., *Re Witty [1913] 2 Ch. 666.*

Application of the Rule against Perpetuities to Various Types of Interests

The rule against perpetuities also applies to subsidiary interests in land, such as powers of appointment, options and other contractual interests.

Effect of Invalidity of an Interest Under the Rule against Perpetuities

Where an interest is void under the rule against perpetuities, it is stricken out; and, subject to the principles established in respect of infectious invalidity, the other interests created in the will or trust instrument take effect as if the void interest had never been provided for.

RULE AGAINST PERPETUAL TRUSTS

The Alienability Policy of the Common Law

The free and liberal circulation of property was recognised early in the development of the common law as one of the inherent rights of a free people. The general policy against the withdrawal of property from commerce has engendered many rules, some of which have already been noted, that promote alienability. Following is a brief sketch of these rules.

Restrictions on alienation contained in grants of freehold estates are regarded unfavourably.[25] One reason for the antipathy against such restrictions has been articulated as follows:— "It is absurd and repugnant to reason that

---

25. See, e.g., Byrne v. Byrne [1953] 87 I.L.T.R. 183, in which a provision that the grantee of a fee simple could not alienate in any circumstances was held invalid; and *Re McDonnell* [1965] I.R. 354, in which a provision that the grantee of a fee simple could not alienate except to a member of the family was held invalid.

he, that hath no possibility to have the land reverted to him, should restrain his feoffee in fee simple of all his power to alien. . . this type of restraint is against the height and puritie of a fee simple."

Restrictions on alienation contained in direct grants of leasehold estates are generally valid at common law. The principal reason is that the lessee does not acquire ownership, of which one of the incidents is the right to alienate. This area of the law has, however, been greatly modified by statute.[26]

The issue of alienability also arises in settlements of property to successive grantees since, of course, the settlement itself constitutes a restriction on alienation for the intermediate holders. The policy favouring alienation is advanced with regard to settlements by the rules governing the remoteness of vesting of future interests; these rules curtail the forms that a settlement can take. One type of settlement, however, is not affected by these rules, namely, the perpetual purpose trust.

The Perpetual Purpose Trust

A purpose trust is one used to promote some particular purpose rather than to benefit some particular individual or class of persons. Such trusts run counter to the general principle that "Every. . . trust (except trusts for charity) must have a definite object. There must be somebody, in whose favour the Court can decree performance".

Nevertheless, there are a number of cases in which purpose trusts have been upheld. Instances are trusts for the erection of tombs or monuments, and trusts for the maintenance of the testator's animals.[27]

---

26. See, e.g., Landlord and Tenant (Amendment) Act, 1980, s. 66.
27. See, e.g., *Re Dean* [1889] 41 Ch. D. 552, a case that involved a bequest unto and to the use of trustees for the use of the testator's dogs and horses for fifty years if any of them should so long live.

A purpose trust, even of the limited kind now allowed, cannot be upheld for an indefinite or perpetual period; such trusts are subject to the rule against perpetual trusts.

Rule against Perpetual Trusts

The rule may be stated as follows:– Property settled in a purpose trust may be directed to be held for the purpose of the trust only for the perpetuity period.[28] Charitable purpose trusts are however exempt from the rule; no gift for charitable purposes, given by way of purpose trust, is void merely because it renders property inalienable in perpetuity. The following is an illustration:– a grant "unto and to the use of T(aker) in fee simple, to the use in perpetuity for the furtherance of sport in Bridge School". The trust is valid, because it is charitable.

RULE AGAINST ACCUMULATION OF INCOME

The rule against accumulations governs the period for which income from property may be accumulated. It restrains the "posthumous avarice" of settlors who may wish to direct the accumulation of income from settled property over too long a period. At common law, the rule is that a direction that income should be accumulated is invalid only if the direction involves accumulation beyond the perpetuity period.

The common law rule against accumulation of income applies in Irish law, subject only to limited modifications made in 1892 respecting directions to accumulate income for the purchase of land.[29]

---

28. See, e.g., *Re Kelly* [1932] I.R. 255.
29. Accumulations Act, 1892.

RULE IN *SHELLEY'S* CASE[30]

The rule may be stated as follows:– "If a freehold is given to a person, and elsewhere within the same document a remainder in fee simple or fee tail is given to the heirs of that person, then that remainder confers a fee simple, or a fee tail, respectively, on the ancestor."

It will be noticed that the operation of the rule is two-fold:– first, it denies to the remainder the effect of a gift to the heirs; secondly, it attributes to the remainder the effect of a gift to the ancestor himself. Therefore, it is "clear that the rule not only defeats the intention (of the settlor) but substitutes a legal intendment directly opposed to the obvious design of the limitation. A rule which so operates cannot be a rule of construction".[31]

The following points merit particular notice. First, the rule applies only if the term "heirs" is used in the plural. In a will the rule may apply when words, such as issue, having the same meaning as heirs or heirs of the body are used. Secondly, the rule applies only if both estates are either legal or equitable. Moreover, the first estate must be freehold. Thirdly, the rule does not apply to executory interests.[32]

The rule, it has been seen, may frustrate the patent intention of a settlor. The rule had a rational basis at its inception, since it assured the rendition of feudal incidents, relief and wardship in particular. It served a purpose even after the decline of feudalism, since it hindered perpetuities. This later rationale for the rule disappeared, however, with the development of alternative and more suitable rules against perpetuities. In modern law, therefore, the rule in Shelley's case is an anachronism.

---

30. [1581] 1 Co. Rep. 886.
31. Haye's Conveyancing 1, 542.
32. See, e.g., *Re Gilbourne* v. *Gilbourne* [1975] Unrep. (H.C., R.I.).

6

Mortgages

MORTGAGE DEFINED

A mortgage is a transaction whereby property is placed as security for the performance of some obligation. The obligation usually consists of the duty to repay money that has been borrowed, together with interest arising on the loan.

Other transactions under which a property may be held as security for the performance of an obligation include the lien, pledge and charge.

IMPORTANCE OF THE MORTGAGE
IN CONVEYANCING PRACTICE

The mortgage arises most frequently in practice in the context of residential property. The reason is that the vast majority of house purchasers proceed by effecting contemporaneously the purchase and a mortgage of the property purchased in order to finance the transaction. It is proposed, therefore, to give special emphasis to mortgage practices in relation to house purchase.

The principal sources of house-purchase finance are building societies, local authorities, assurance companies and banks. Building societies and local authorities are long established sources of long-term financing in this area. Insurance companies have in recent years provided long-term financing facilities as an adjunct service to the business of providing insurance. Banks, until recent years, were of minor importance as sources of long-term house-purchase finance. They have traditionally, however, been the principal sources of short-term finance, i.e., "bridging accommodation".

The lending institutions employ various rationing or queue devices in rationing available funds when the demand for house-purchase finance exceeds supply. A building society may, for instance, advance funds only to an applicant who has been a member of the society. Rationing of local authority house-purchase finance is carried out principally by means of an income test, i.e., loans are advanced only to candidates whose income does not exceed a certain level.

The financial institutions employ various criteria – apart from those concerned with rationing – in assessing a loan application. The two principal factors considered are the candidate's ability to repay and the value of the property available as security.

(a) Ability to Repay

A variety of considerations are relevant in assessing this factor. These include the candidate's personal standing, the amount of his income and the nature of his employment, for instance, whether it is permanent or temporary. The income of the candidate's spouse may also be considered when it derives from an employment that is permanent and pensionable.

A candidate's income is also relevant to the question of the amount of the loan to be advanced. A rule-of-thumb that is commonly followed is that the amount of any loan advanced should not be such that the annual repayments would exceed twenty five percent of the candidate's income.

(b) *Value of the Property Available as Security*

Conservative valuations of the property are adopted. For instance, the lower figure is taken where there is a difference between the market value of the property and the price paid for it by a loan candidate.

The valuation made of a property is relevant to the question of the amount to be advanced as well as to the question of whether or not to make the advance. Loans for house-purchase are usually restricted in amount to seventy five percent approximately of the valuation of the property available as security. Local authorities, by way of exception, are normally prepared to lend to approximately ninety per cent of the valuation.

The foregoing discussion has concerned the availability of loan funds to the individual purchaser. Different considerations apply to the availability of credit to the property developer. Banks have been the principal source of such credit.

A banker, to whom a development project has been presented for assessment, will be concerned with the following points in particular:–

(a) The qualifications and experience of the developer,

(b) The equity capital of the developer – banks will normally require that he be able to furnish between twenty and fifty per cent of the total cost,

(c) Proof of the existence of a demand for the proposed development, for instance, evidence of a demand for office space where an office block is proposed,

(d) Evidence of approval from local authorities for the development,

(e) A detailed costing of the project, and

(f) Proof of the competence and reputation of the experts, such as the architects and engineers, engaged for the project.

CREATION OF MORTGAGES

The methods available for encumbering real property by mortgage vary depending on a variety of factors. These include:– the nature of the property, i.e., freehold or leasehold; the title of the property, i.e., registered or unregistered; and the borrower's interest in the property, i.e., legal or equitable.

These methods will be considered under the general headings of Legal Mortgages and Equitable Mortgages.

Consideration of the methods of effecting a mortgage must be prefaced by a comment on the influence of Equity in this area. It is established that the interpretation of a transaction as a mortgage depends not alone on the form used, but also on the intent of the parties. For instance, a transaction will be interpreted as a mortgage, even though in the form of an absolute conveyance, if such was the intent of the parties.[1]

LEGAL MORTGAGES

Unregistered Freehold

Two methods exist for creating a legal mortgage in respect of unregistered freehold property. These are a conveyance in fee simple of the property subject to a proviso for redemption and, secondly, a lease of the property subject to a proviso for cesser. These methods will be considered in turn.

1. First, a legal mortgage over unregistered freehold property can be created by a conveyance of the fee simple subject to a proviso for redemption by repayment on the

---

1. See, e.g., *Salt* v. *Marquess of Northampton* [1892] A.C. 1.

legal date of redemption. This date is set at a short period
– normally one month – from the date of the mortgage. The
mortgagor's right to redeem on this date is referred to as
the legal right of redemption.

The mortgagor becomes entitled to an equity of redemption – which includes an equitable power to redeem
– after the legal date of redemption has passed. The influence of Equity here has indeed negated the importance of
the legal date of redemption, and it is seldom that parties
to a mortgage contemplate legal redemption.

2. A second method of creating a mortgage over unregistered freehold is to lease the property for a term of years
to the lender. The lease will contain a proviso for cesser of
the term of years.

This method is less common than the conveyance subject to a proviso for redemption. It can, however, be used
to advantage where:– (A) the freehold is a fee farm grant –
the lender may not wish to be liable for the fee farm rent;
or (B) the borrower wishes to reserve the option of creating
further legal mortgages.

Unregistered Leasehold

Legal mortgages in respect of unregistered leasehold
can be created either by assignment or by sub-demise.
Where the mortgage is by assignment, it will be subject to
a proviso for redemption on repayment.

It is more common to create mortgages over unregistered leasehold by sub-demise. The sub-lease will be subject
to a proviso for cesser on redemption. Sub-demise has two
advantages over assignment as a method of mortgaging
unregistered leasehold. First, it avoids the creation of
privity of contract between the borrower's lessor and the
lender. Secondly, it enables the borrower to retain the
option of creating further legal mortgages by sub-demise.

EQUITABLE MORTGAGES

There are three methods of creating an equitable mortgage over property. These are by:– 1. an agreement to create a legal mortgage; 2. a deposit of title deeds as security for a loan; and 3. the mortgage of an equitable interest in property. These methods are valid regardless of whether the property is freehold or leasehold.

1. *Agreement to Create a Legal Mortgage*

An agreement to create a legal mortgage operates to create an equitable mortgage.[2] The agreement should be in compliance with section 2 of the Statute of Frauds (Ir.), 1695, or, alternatively, be supported by a sufficient act of part performance such as the advancement of part or all of the loan.[3] Instances of mortgages arising in this way are very rare.

2. *Deposit of Title Deeds as Security For a Loan*

Creation of an equitable mortgage in this way has a number of advantages for the mortgagor. First, the costs are considerably reduced since no stamp duty is payable and there will be no document requiring registration in the Registry of Deeds. Secondly, a purchaser who is purchasing with a view to re-sale may prefer not to have to produce a mortgage release deed as one of the title documents on the re-sale.

Conversely, this method of creating mortgages has disadvantages for the mortgagee. First, the rights of an equitable mortgagee are less extensive than those of a legal mortgagee. Secondly, any ambiguity in relation to the

---

2. See, e.g., *Eyre* v. *McDowell* [1861] 9 H.L.C. 619.
3. See, e.g., *Sichel* v. *Mosenthal* [1862] 30 Beav. 371.

purpose of a deposit will be construed against the depositee.[4] In consequence, the practice has developed of issuing a receipt containing particulars of a deposit and to require the depositor to give a receipt for such receipt.

Instances of mortgages arising in this way are rare. Local Authorities are in fact prohibited by regulations from lending on a mortgage by deposit of title deeds, except in a limited class of cases. Other institutions that lend on mortgage rarely depart from their standard practice of refusing such security, and will so depart only if the borrower's personal standing is good and the title to the property available as security is beyond question.

3. Mortgage of an Equitable Interest in Property

A person lacking a legal interest in property – such as a person who has previously conveyed a freehold on mortgage or a beneficiary under a trust – can offer only an equitable interest as security for a loan. It should be created by deed or in writing.

Instances of this type of mortgage are again very rare because of the reluctance of lending institutions to lend on an equitable interest. The regulations of most of these institutions in fact prohibit the acceptance of such security. The practice of banks is more flexible in this respect; some banks will lend on this type of security where the borrower is in good standing, is unable to offer alternative security and has a reasonable equity in the property.

Supplementary Points on the Creation of Mortgages

Brief reference can be made to two further topics in the creation of mortgages, namely, sub-mortgages and

---

4. See, e.g., *Northern Bank Co. Ltd.* v. *Carpenter* [1931] I.R. 268; and *National Bank* v. *McGovern* [1931] I.R. 368.

mortgages in respect of registered property.

A sub-mortgage is a mortgage of a mortgagee's interest. It is created by a mortgagee conveying his estate and assigning the mortgage debt to a sub-mortgagee subject to a proviso for redemption.

A legal mortgage can be created over either freehold or leasehold property, the title to which is registered in the Land Registry, by registering the mortgage as a burden on the title.[5] An equitable mortgage, similarly, may be created over such property by the mortgagor depositing the land certificate or certificate of charge with the mortgagee.[6]

MORTGAGEE'S RIGHTS, POWERS AND REMEDIES

A mortgagee acquires an extensive range of rights against the mortgagor. Many of these rights are directed at the situation where a mortgagor has defaulted with repayments.

It must be stated, however, that it is only in the exceptional case that lending institutions find it necessary to exercise these rights. The attitude taken is that "prevention is better than cure". Consequently, lending institutions minimize the incidence of defaults by the adoption of cautious and conservative policies in processing loan applications.

1. *Rights to Sue on the Personal Covenant for Repayment*

A mortgagee can sue on the personal covenant for repayment if the mortgagor is in arrears with repayments

---

5. Registration of Title Act, 1964, s. 62.
6. Registration of Title Act, 1964, s. 105(6). This provision states that the deposit must be for the purpose of creating a lien on the property to which the land certificate relates.

either of capital or interest, so long as the debt has not become statute barred.

This right is used in practice to achieve one of two different objectives. First, it may be used immediately that a default has taken place as a stimulant to repayment. Secondly, it may be used to recover any deficit outstanding after the mortgagee has exercised other remedies, such as sale of the security, against the mortgagor.

It is generally stated that the remedies available to a mortgagee are cumulative. There are, however, dicta to the effect that one may not join an action on the personal covenant for repayment with an application for an order permitting sale of the security in the same summary summons.[7]

2. *Right to Possession*

A legal mortgagee has the theoretical right to possession of the mortgaged property upon creation of the mortgage. An equitable mortgagee's right to possession is doubtful, although it is clear that a court may in the exercise of its discretion grant an order for possession to such a mortgagee.[8]

The exercise of the right to possession immediately upon the creation of a mortgage will in almost all cases be against the spirit of a mortgage created over residential property. A Welch mortgage is an exception. The understanding under such a mortgage is that the mortgagee will enter possession and set off the rents or profits issuing from the property against the repayments.[9]

A mortgagee, although theoretically entitled to possession, will frequently require a court order to obtain it. Moreover, a court may in the exercise of its discretion refuse

---

7. See, e.g., *Barden* v. *Downes* [1940] I.R. 131.
8. See, e.g., *National Bank* v. *Shanahan* [1932] 66 I.L.T.R. 120.
9. See, e.g., *Shields* v. *Shields* [1904] 38 I.L.T.R. 188.

an order for possession.[10]

The basic objective in obtaining possession will be to secure repayment of the capital and interest. Re-possession in itself achieves this objective only when an adequate rental income issues from the property. Consequently, lending institutions normally view the remedy of possession merely as a prelude to the exercise of some other remedy, such as a sale of the security, against the borrower.

A mortgagee who enters possession incurs certain obligations to the mortgagor. In particular, the property must be managed in a business-like manner and any excess of the income from the property over the repayment instalments due must be paid to the mortgagor.[11]

3. Right to Sell

A mortgagee has no power to sell at law or in equity. Any power of sale must derive either from:– first, an express provision in the mortgage, secondly, an order of the court, or thirdly, section 19 of the Conveyancing Act, 1881, as amended by the Conveyancing Act 1911.[12]

The statutory power of sale arises when:– (1) the mortgage is by deed, and (2) the mortgage money has become due. The statutory power becomes exerciseable when:–

a. written notice requesting payment is made and there is a three months default, or

b. some interest under the mortgage is two months in arrears, or

---

10. See, e.g., *National Bank* v. *Shanahan* [1932] 66 I.L.T.R. 120.
11. See, e.g., *White* v. *City of London Brewery Co.* [1889] 42 Ch. D. 237.
12. See, e.g., *Bank of Ireland* v. *Waldrow* [1944] I.R. 303.

c. the mortgagor is in breach of some condition implied by the Conveyancing Acts or contained in the mortgage deed other than the covenant for the payment of principal or interest.

It has been stated that, in Ireland, sale as distinct from foreclosure is the proper remedy for a mortgagee.[13] Lending institutions customarily exercise their power of sale only after the action on the personal covenant for repayment has failed to secure payment.

A mortgagee should proceed to obtain possession where mortgaged property is being sold with vacant possession. This applies even when the sale is being carried out under a court order.[14]

A valid sale vests the mortgaged property in the purchaser free from the mortgagor's equity of redemption.

It is settled that Irish courts have "jurisdiction to decree foreclosure and not sale in a mortgagee's suit, but will only exercise such jurisdiction in exceptional circumstances".[15] In a later case it was noted that proceedings in Ireland "are for sale and never for foreclosure".[16]

Should foreclosure be ordered, the practice in English law indicates that a court will normally make a foreclosure order nisi on foot of an application for foreclosure. A foreclosure order absolute will later be made if the mortgagor or subsequent mortgagees do not avail of the stay in the order by redeeming the interest of the mortgagee applying for foreclosure. Even after a foreclosure order absolute has been made, a court may "open" the foreclosure in certain circumstances. Finally, where there are several mortgagees interested in foreclosing on a mortgaged property, their

---

13. See, e.g., *Barden* v. *Downes* [1940] I.R. 131.
14. *Bank of Ireland* v. *Waldrow* [1944] I.R. 303.
15. See, e.g., *Bruce* v. *Brophy* [1906] 1 I.R. 611.
16. *Barden* v. *Downes* [1940] I.R. 131.

respective rights are determined by the rule "redeem up, foreclose down".

5. *Right to Appoint a Receiver*

The law relating to the sources of a mortgagee's power to appoint a receiver, and to the times when such a power arises and becomes exerciseable, is the same as that relating to a mortgagee's power to sell.[17]

This right to appoint a receiver is almost never exercised over residential property – the exceptional case is where an adequate rental issues from the property. Viewed as an alternative to entering possession, the appointment of a receiver has the advantage that the receiver is deemed to be the agent of the mortgagor.[18]

A receiver should be appointed in writing. Unless expressly given more power, a receiver's only powers are to collect the rent and profits issuing from the property and to distribute these in the following order:– first, in discharge of outgoings; secondly, in servicing loans having priority to the mortgage; thirdly, in payment of his commission, insurance premiums and for any repairs authorised; fourthly, in payment of the interest under the mortgage; fifthly, if the mortgagee so directs in writing, towards the discharge of the principal money lent – otherwise it must be paid to the person who would have received it if the receiver had not been appointed, i.e., normally the mortgagor.[19]

A receiver may exercise any additional powers delegated to him by the mortgagee. Additional powers could include powers of insuring, repairing, leasing or of accepting surrenders of leases of the mortgaged property.

---

17. Conveyancing Act, 1881, ss. 19(1) and 20.
18. Conveyancing Act, 1881, s. 24.
19. Conveyancing Act, 1881, ss. 24(3) and 24(8).

6. Right to Grant Leases

The right to grant leases is another remedy that may be available to a mortgagee where repayments are in arrears. This remedy is almost never exercised over residential property – an exceptional case is where an attempt to sell the property has failed.

A mortgagee has no power to grant leases that will bind the mortgagor at law or in equity. Any power to grant such leases must derive from either:– first, the mortgage itself; secondly, the consent of the mortgagor in a particular case; or thirdly, section 18 of the Conveyancing Act, 1881.

The statutory power to grant leases is highly regulated as follows:– first, it can be exercised only by a mortgagee in possession, actual or constructive – as, for instance, where a receiver has been appointed; secondly, the terms of leases made under the statute cannot exceed twenty one years in the case of agricultural or occupational leases or ninety nine years in the case of building leases; and thirdly, such leases must comply with the following conditions:–

1. they must be limited to take effect not later than twelve months after their execution;

2. the best rent reasonably obtainable must be reserved;

3. they must contain "a condition of re-entry on the rent not being paid within a period therein specified, not exceeding thirty days",[20] and

4. counterparts of any such lease must be executed by the lessee and delivered to the lessor.

7. Right to Accept Surrenders of Leases

The power of a mortgagee to accept a surrender of a lease over mortgaged property must derive from either:–

---

20. In *Murphy and Co. Ltd.* v. *Marren* [1933] I.R. 393, it was held that this provision also applies to letting agreements made under the statutory power.

first, the mortgage itself; secondly, the consent of the mortgagor in a particular case; or thirdly, section 3 of the Conveyancing Act, 1911.

The statutory power to accept surrender may be exercised only by a mortgagee who is in possession, and may be exercised only in order that a new lease be granted. Leases granted after the acceptance of a surrender must comply with certain conditions. These conditions are designed to ensure that the profitability of the mortgaged property under the new lease will be at least as great as under the surrendered lease.

8. Right to Insure

A mortgagee has the right to insure the mortgaged property against fire at the mortgagor's expense in the case of every mortgage created by deed.[21] This right may be excluded or modified by express agreement – it is quite common for a mortgage to reserve a right to insure that is more extensive than the statutory right.

The amount of the insurance must not exceed the amount, if any, specified in the deed or, where no amount is specified, two-thirds of the amount that would be necessary to restore the property in the event of its total destruction.[22] The implied statutory right is excluded if:– first, the mortgage deed excludes it; or secondly, the mortgagor maintains insurance where required to do so by the mortgagee deed; or thirdly, the mortgage deed is silent as to insurance and the mortgagor maintains insurance up to the statutory limit with the mortgagee's consent.

9. Right to Possession of Title Deeds

A first mortgagee has a right to possession of the title

---

21. Conveyancing Act, 1881, s. 19.
22. Conveyancing Act, 1881, s. 23(1).

deeds.

A mortgagee in possession of title deeds has a duty to take reasonable care in relation to them, and may be made liable to the mortgagor for any damage resulting from their loss or destruction.[23]

A mortgagor may inspect and copy the deeds at any reasonable time upon payment of the mortgagee's expenses. A mortgagor is entitled to repossess the title deeds upon redemption.[24]

10. Right to Fixtures

Whether or not fixtures form part of the secured property depends upon the interpretation of a mortgage deed. Nevertheless, there appears to be a presumption that all fixtures attached before the date of the mortgage are comprised in the secured property.[25] In Irish law, there appears to be a presumption that any fixtures attached after the date of the mortgage are not comprised in the security.[26]

11. Right to Consolidate

Equity courts developed the mortgagee's right of consolidation. The right as it existed before the Conveyancing Act, 1881, may be described as follows:– "A mortgagee, who holds several distinct mortgages under the same mortgagor, redeemable, not by express contract, but only by virtue of the equity of redemption, may consolidate them, i.e., treat them as one, decline to be redeemed as to any, unless he is redeemed as to all."

Since section 17 of the Conveyancing Act, 1881, a mortgagee retains a right of consolidation only if one of the mortgage deeds to which he is a party expressly reserves the right.

---

23. See, e.g., *Gilligan* v. *National Bank Ltd.* [1901] 2 I.R. 513.
24. Conveyancing Act, 1881, s. 16(1).
25. See, e.g., in *Re James Calvert* [1898] 2 I.R. 501.
26. In *Re James Calvert* [1898] 2 I.R. 501.

The mortgagee's right of consolidation may prejudice a person who purchases mortgaged property from a mortgagor. The right is not much favoured in Irish law.[27]

12. *Right to Stay Out of Mortgagor's Bankruptcy Proceedings*

A mortgagee is a secured creditor, and may stay outside bankruptcy proceedings of the mortgagor.

The mortgagee's right exists only if the mortgage was not effected to defraud creditors or was not otherwise in violation of the Bankruptcy Act, 1988.

13. *Right to Tack Further Advances*

This right will be considered briefly in connection with priority as between mortgages.[28]

14. *Miscellaneous Rights*

A mortgagee has the following miscellaneous rights:— first, a right to sue for an accounting; secondly, a right to sue for a declaration of right; and thirdly, a right to compel the mortgagor to protect mortgaged property against trespassers, for instance, persons acquiring title by adverse possession under the Statute of Limitations, 1957.

MORTGAGOR'S RIGHTS, POWERS AND REMEDIES

1. *Right to Redeem*

A mortgagor has a legal right to redeem the mortgage on the date set for legal redemption. A mortgagor may

---

27. See, e.g., *Gore-Hickman* v. *Alliance Assurance Co. Ltd.*, [1936] I.R. 721.
28. See infra at page 83.

redeem prior to the date set for legal redemption if the mortgagee has entered possession.[29]

A mortgagor may redeem after the legal redemption date by virtue of his equitable right to redeem.[30] A mortgagor redeeming under the equitable right to redeem should however give notice of his intention to redeem to the mortgagee, or interest in lieu thereof, insofar as reasonable provision for such has been agreed, unless the mortgagee has entered possession or taken other steps to enforce the security.[31]

It may be noted that any person having an interest in the equity of redemption, such as assignees or lessees – and not only mortgagors – are entitled to redeem.[32]

Courts zealously protect a mortgagor's rights of redemption and have established the following rules in order to protect these rights:–

First, Equity looks at the intent and not to the form in deciding whether the parties intend a mortgage as distinct from an outright conveyance.

Secondly, Equity treats as invalid any provision in a mortgage that clogs the right to redeem.[33] A mortgagor may however, in a transaction subsequent to and independent of the mortgage, dispose of the redemption right. Moreover, a mortgagor's legal right to redeem may be postponed for a reasonable period of time.[34]

Thirdly, Equity permits the mortgagor to redeem the secured property free from any unfair or repressive

---

29. See, e.g., *Crickmore* v. *Freeston* [1870] 40 L.J. Ch. 137.
30. See, e.g., *Browne* v. *Ryan* [1901] 2 I.R. 653.
31. See, e.g., *Smith* v. *Smith* [1891] 3 Ch. 550.
32. See, e.g., *Pearce* v. *Morris* [1869] 5 Ch. App. 227.
33. See, e.g., *Fairclough* v. *Swan Brewery Co. Ltd.* [1912] A.C. 565.
34. See, e.g., Knightbridge Estates T. Ltd. v. Byrne [1939] Ch. 441. [C.A.].

restrictions.[35]

2. *Right to the Rent and Profits of the Mortgaged Property*

A mortgagor has the above right together with the ancillary right to sue for such rents and profits in his own name under the Judicature Act, 1887.

3. *Miscellaneous Rights*

A mortgagor has similar rights to a mortgagee in relation to both the granting of leases and the acceptance of surrenders of leases.

The right of a mortgagor to inspect and copy the title documents to the mortgaged property has been discussed previously.[36]

PRIORITY BETWEEN MORTGAGES

Unregistered Mortgages

Priority as between unregistered mortgages is governed by two main principles. First, earlier mortgages have priority over later mortgages. Secondly, legal mortgages have priority over equitable mortgages.

A conflict between two unregistered mortgages may fall into one of four classes:– (A) two legal mortgages; (B) first legal mortgage and later equitable mortgage; (C) first equitable mortgage and later legal mortgage; and (D) two equitable mortgages. Any such conflict will be resolved by reference to the principles set out above.

---

35. See, e.g., *Bradley* v. *Carritt* [1903] A.C. 253; and *Kreglinger* v. *New Patagonia Meat & Cold Storage Co. Ltd.* [1914] A.C. 25.
36. See supra at pages 78 and 79.

Doctrine of Tacking

Tacking is a special way of obtaining priority for a secured loan by amalgamating it with another secured loan of higher priority. The following are illustrations:– First, in a conflict between two equitable mortgagees, the later may gain priority over the earlier by acquiring a legal mortgage that has priority to both. Secondly, the priority given to a mortgagee who has the legal estate extends to subsequent advances made by him, provided he is unaware of other mortgages when he makes these advances.

Impact of the Registration of Deeds Act, 1707

The foregoing rules governing priority are normally precluded in relation to unregistered land by the operation of the Registration of Deeds Act, 1707. That Act introduced the system of registration of deeds.[37] It provides that priority, as between two or more deeds that create conflicting interests, may be determined by registration of one of the deeds. Priority under the Act is determined by reference to the dates of registration of deeds.

JUDGEMENT MORTGAGES

A form of statutory mortgage can be created under the Judgement Mortgage Act, 1850. Any judgement creditor may, under that Act, make an affidavit specifying any lands of which his judgment debtor is seised or possessed, or over which the judgement debtor has an unfettered general power of appointment.[38]

Registration of the affidavit vests all the estate of the judgement debtor in the lands specified in the judgement creditor, subject to the former's right of redemption on

---

37. See, infra, Chapter 17 at page 214 et seq.
38. Judgement Mortgage (Ireland) Act, 1850, s. 6.

payment of the judgement debt.

The Act therefore allows a judgement debt to be converted into a judgement mortgage over the debtor's realty. The rights and remedies of a judgement mortgagee are theoretically the same as those of a mortgagee by deed. In practice, however, the usual remedy of a judgement mortgagee is sale under a court order.

7

Easements and Profits

Theories of absolute ownership of land are obsolete. A person's enjoyment of land is invariably restricted by encumbrances existing in favour of other persons. The particular categories of encumbrances for present consideration are easements and profits.

EASEMENT DEFINED

An easement is a right of an owner of real property in respect of another's land. One can readily point to many familar instances of easements – the right to place pipe lines under another's land, the right to use a path across another's land, and the right to flood another's land.

An easement may be positive, such as a right of way; or it may be negative, such as a right to light. Easements can be acquired both by and against limited owners of property, such as, weekly tenants.[1] The dominant tenement may consist of corporeal property such as land, or of incorporeal property such as a profit.

PREREQUISITES TO EASEMENTS

There are four prerequisites to the existence of an easement, as follows:–

---

1. See, e.g., *Tallon* v. *Ennis* [1937] I.R. 549.

First, a dominant and a servient tenement must exist. The rule is sometimes expressed by saying that an easement cannot be enjoyed "in gross".[2]

Secondly, the easement as an encumbrance on the servient tenement must accommodate the dominant tenement. It is not sufficient that the owner of the dominant tenement be accommodated only in a personal capacity.[3]

Thirdly, an easement cannot exist where the dominant tenement and the servient tenement are both owned and occupied by the same person; in this situation, there can be what is referred to as a "quasi-easement".

Fourthly, a right, to qualify as an easement, must be capable of forming the subject matter of a grant. This is a corollary of the rule that all easements, even those arising by prescription, are presumed to lie in grant.[4] Three distinct aspects of this fourth prerequisite are as follows:–

    a. The right claimed as an easement must be sufficiently defined,

    b. The grantor must have capacity to make the grant, and

    c. the grantee must have capacity to take the grant.

ACQUISITION OF EASEMENTS

Having considered the outer limits of the category of rights that can qualify as easements, it is now proposed to discuss how an easement may be acquired. In general terms, an easement can be acquired by grant, reservation, prescription or statute.

---

2. See, e.g., *Hawkins* v. *Rutter* [1892] 1 Q.B. 668.
3. See, e.g., *Hill* v. *Tupper* [1863] 2 H. & C. 121.
4. See, e.g., *Cochrane* v. *Verner* [1895] 29 I.L.J. 571.

1. *Express Grant or Reservation*

The major question here concerns the formal requirements necessary to establish an easement through express grant or reservation. Three points can be made. First, the grant or reservation should be by deed or in writing.[5] Secondly, absence of these formalities may not be fatal – for instance, a claimant to an express grant or reservation may rely on estoppel.[6] Thirdly, a conveyance of land passes together with other privileges attached to the land any easements enjoyed in respect of it.

A subsidiary question concerns the necessary procedure to be adopted by a person who wishes to expressly reserve an easement over a portion of property that is being disposed of. The reservation should either be executed by the grantee of the property or, alternatively, be made by a conveyance to uses. The rationale is that an easement is presumed to lie in grant.

2. *Implied Grant or Reservation*

It may be impossible to establish an easement by express grant or reservation. The question of an easement may never have arisen between neighbouring property owners. Alternatively, an attempt may have been made to expressly create an easement, but the attempt may have failed through a failure to use adequate formalities or proper procedures. Nevertheless, something in the fact situation pertaining between neighbouring property owners may imply that an easement was granted or reserved between them.

Easements by implied grant may be based on any of the following doctrines:–

---

5. These are requirements of the common law and of the Statute of Frauds, respectively.
6. See, e.g., *Annally Hotel Ltd.* v. *Bergin* [1970] 1 I.L.T.R. 6.

1. *Necessity*. The claimant contends that some right over adjacent property is essential to the enjoyment of his own;[7]

2. *Intention*. The basis of the claim will be that the owners of adjacent properties intended a right to subsist over one of the holdings for the benefit of the other;[8] or

3. *Wheeldon v. Burrows.*[9] This doctrine provides that, on the disposal of part of a holding, quasi-easements may be converted into easements in favour of the grantee. This conversion occurs if the quasi-easements:– (a) were continuous and apparent, or (b) necessary to the reasonable enjoyment of the land granted and in either case, (c) had been, and were at the time of the grant, used by the grantor for the benefit of the part granted.[10]

Easements by implied reservation may be based on doctrines either of:–

4. *Necessity*, or
5. *Intention*.

The foregoing analysis refers to the position where an owner has disposed only of one portion of a property; it sets out the doctrines under which the purchaser can claim an implied grant of an easement and under which the disposing owner can claim an implied reservation of an easement.

One may now consider the position where the disposing owner disposes of another portion of the property. On

---

7. See, e.g., *Browne* v. *Maguire* [1922] 1 I.R. 23.
8. See, e.g., *Donnelly* v. *Adams* [1905] 1 I.R. 157.
9. [1879] 12 Ch. D. 31.
10. See, e.g., *McDonagh* v. *Mulholland* [1931] I.R. 110.

what doctrines can the second purchaser rely in claiming an implied easement against the first purchaser? The answer depends on whether or not the second disposition takes place simultaneously with the first disposition. Where the two dispositions are simultaneous, the second purchaser can rely on the doctrine of intention referred to above. Where the second disposition takes place at a later date than the first, the second purchaser can rely on the doctrines of either necessity or intention already referred to.

3. Prescription

An easement may be acquired by prescription, i.e., by long enjoyment of a right. Resort to prescription is made only when no grant, express or implied, of an easement can be proved. Prescription, however, presumes that a grant was made at some time.

Prescription of an easement may be claimed at common law, under the doctrine of the lost modern grant or under the Prescription (Ireland) Act, 1858. These will be considered in turn.

A. Common Law Prescription

A claimant must prove user from time immemorial, i.e., 1189. In practice, proof of user for even twenty years may suffice.[11]

B. Prescription under the Doctrine of the Lost Modern Grant

A court, under this doctrine, will presume a modern grant as long as user can be shown – here again, a twenty year period of user may suffice.[12]

---

11. See, e.g., *Bailey* v. *Appleyard* [1839] 8 A. & E. 161.
12. See, e.g., *Bryant* v. *Foot* [1868] I.R. 3 Q.B. 497; and *Tisdall* v. *McArthur & Co. (S. & M.) Ltd.* [1951] I.R. 228.

C. *Statutory Prescription under the 1858 Act*[13]

A claimant, in order to establish a prescriptive right to an easement under statute, must show "uninterrupted user as of right for either twenty or forty years, which periods must directly precede any litigation as to the existence of the easement".[14]

"Interruption of user", as used in the Act, is a term of art. It means an obstruction of the right claimed, which obstruction is acquiesced in by the owner of the dominant tenement for at least a year. The erection of an unlocked gate has been held not to constitute an obstruction to a right of way.[15]

It is necessary, in computing the claim periods, to deduct any periods during which the owner of the servient tenement was under a disability. The term "disability" has different meanings depending upon whether a claim is based on the twenty years or on the forty years period of user. In relation to claims based on a twenty year period of user, a servient owner is regarded as under a disability while an infant, a lunatic or a life tenant.[16] In relation to claims based on a forty year period of user, a servient owner is regarded as under a disability while a life tenant or while holding for a term exceeding three years.[17]

Finally, it can be noted that the Prescription Act does not apply to rights to air or to support, and also that the Act contains special provisions on the right to light.[18]

---

13. The Prescription (Ireland) Act, 1858, adapted the provisions of the Prescription Act, 1832, to Ireland.
14. Prescription Act, 1832, ss. 1 and 2.
15. See, e.g., *Flynn* v. *Harte* [1913] 2 I.R. 322.
16. Prescription Act, 1832, s. 7.
17. Prescription Act, 1832, s. 8.
18. See, infra, at pages 92 to 94.

Defences to Prescriptive Claims

A number of defences are available against prescriptive claims. These defences derive from common law, but have been modified in relation to statutory prescriptive claims by the Prescription Act, 1858.

1. General Defences

The owner of a servient tenement may resist a claim to a prescribed easement by proving any of the following:

    a. that any of the four prerequisites to an easement was lacking during the period of user relied on, or
    b. that the user was forcible (vi), secret (clam) or permissive (precario), or
    c. that the user was not continuous.

2. Defences to Statutory Prescriptive Claims

The general defences to prescriptive claims apply with certain modifications to statutory prescriptive claims.

First, a statutory prescriptive claim to an easement based on a twenty year period will fail if it is shown that the user was permissive, irrespective of whether the permission was given verbally or in writing. Similarly, a statutory prescriptive claim to an easement based on a forty year period will fail if it is shown that the user was permissive, but only if the permission was given in writing or, if given verbally, was renewed annually.[19]

Secondly, the defence that the user was not continuous – applicable to the two other methods of prescription – assumes a different form in relation to statutory prescription. The defence here is that a claim was "with interruption".

---

19. See, e.g., *Gardner* v. *Hodgson's Kingston Brewery Co. Ltd.* [1903] A.C. 229.

4. *Statute*

Statutes may create easements as defined, or rights analogous to easements. The latter include, for instance, rights given to public bodies in respect of the erection or installation of telegraph poles and wires, electric cables, and gas and water pipes.

THE EASEMENT OF LIGHT

A. *Acquisition*

One can acquire an easement of light by grant or reservation in the same way that one can acquire any other type of easement.

The acquisition of an easement of light by common law or lost modern grant prescription is however more difficult than for other easements. Conversely, an easement of light is the easement most easily acquired by statutory prescription.

Section 3 of the Prescription Act, 1858, provides as follows:–

> "Actual enjoyment of the access of light to a dwelling-house, workshop or other building for twenty years without interruption shall make the right absolute and indefeasible, unless enjoyed by written consent or agreement."

The general effect of the section is to make twenty years enjoyment of light equal to forty years enjoyment of any other right, subject to the following qualifications:–

1. User as of right is unnecessary. Verbal consent, though evidenced by annual payments, is no bar.
2. The disabilities of infancy, lunacy, life term or term of years exceeding three years, cannot be pleaded.
3. Unity of possession of the dominant and servient

tenements in the period next before action does not vitiate a claim under the Act – it merely suspends the running of the period.

Except as aforesaid, the elements of a statutory prescriptive claim to an easement of light are similar to those for other easements. Thus, the twenty years period must be the next before action.[20] Also, interruption has the same special meaning as in other cases. It means some hostile obstruction, even by a stranger, lasting for at least a year.[21]

B. Scope of Acquired Easement of Light

Questions on the scope of acquired easements arise frequently. For instance, a person who has acquired a prescriptive right to walk across another's land may not be entitled to drive across that land.

Much of the litigation on the easement of light has focused on the extent of the right acquired. The courts have adopted a flexible approach in setting out guidelines on what constitutes an actionable interference with the easement.[22]

Thus, ordinary light is to be interpreted in a common sense manner, and not by reference to rigid expert tests such as the forty five degree rule.[23] Also, the sufficiency of the quantum left in relation to the quantum originally enjoyed is an important factor in gauging an actionable interference.[24]

Finally, tests based on physics, such as the grumble point test, are viewed with reserve. A safer guideline is whether there is a substantial diminution of light – the most

---

20. See, e.g., *Hyman v. Van Den Bergh* [1907] 2 Ch. 500.
21. See. e.g., *Smith v. Baxter* [1900] 2 Ch. 138.
22. See, e.g., *Colls v. Home and Colonial Stores Ltd.* [1904] A.C. 179.
23. See, e.g., *Smith v. Dublin Theatre Co.* [1936] I.R. 692.
24. See, e.g., *Gannon v. Hughes* [1937] I.R. 284.

reliable evidence is normally provided by those who know the property.[25]

RELATIONSHIP BETWEEN DOMINANT AND SERVIENT OWNERS

Disputes may still arise between a dominant and servient owner after the existence of an easement has been established. Two common areas of dispute concern the scope of the acquired easement, and also the liability for maintaining it. The relevant precepts governing these matters will now be considered.

First, the dominant owner is entitled to enjoy the easement, free from interference either by the servient owner or by any third party. The scope of the acquired easement is of course critical to the question of whether a particular act or omission constitutes an interference with it.

Secondly, the general rule is that a servient owner is not liable to maintain an easement.[26] The policy of the law is indeed against recognition of any easement that would involve the servient owner in financial expenditure. There are, however, two exceptional cases. Thus, an easement requiring a servient owner to fence land in order to keep out cattle has been recognised.[27] Also, a grant of an easement may stipulate that the servient owner be liable for maintenance.[28]

Thirdly, a dominant owner is under no liability for normal wear and tear of an easement.[29] A grant of an easement, moreover, may specifically exempt a dominant

---

25. See, e.g., *McGrath* v. *Munster & Leinster Bank Ltd.* [1959] I.R. 313.
26. See, e.g., *Kelly* v. *Dea* [1966] 100 I.L.T.R. 1.
27. See, e.g., *Lawrence* v. *Jenkins* [1873] L.R. 8 A.B. 244.
28. See, e.g., *Gaw* v. *C.I.E.* [1953] I.R. 232.
29. See, e.g., *Cleary* v. *Bohen* [1931] L.J. I.R. 148.

owner from repairing liability.[30] A dominant owner may however be made liable in trespass or nuisance for "excessive user".

Fourthly, a dominant owner, although under no duty to do so, has a right to maintain an easement. Moreover, he may enter the servient property, insofar as this is necessary, to effect the maintenance.[31]

Finally, both dominant and servient owners can enforce their respective rights by action.

EXTINGUISHMENT OF EASEMENTS

Following are the principal ways in which an easement terminates, thereby restoring the servient owner to unburdened possession of his or her property.

1. *Express Release*

A dominant owner may expressly release a servient tenement from the encumbrance of an easement. The release should be by deed or in writing, although an informal release may be effective under estoppel principles.[32]

2. *Implied Release*

A dominant owner may impliedly release an easement. An intention to release an easement may be found if the dominant owner has:–

   a. Abandoned the easement.[33] Nonuser without more does not, however, constitute an abandonment;

---

30. See, e.g., *Griffin* v. *Keane* [1927] 61 I.L.T.R. 177.
31. See, e.g., *Kelly* v. *Dea* [1966] 100 I.L.T.R. 1.
32. See, e.g., *Davies* v. *Marshall* [1861] 10 C.B. [N.S.] 697.
33. See, e.g., *Stevenson* v. *Parke* [1932] L.J. I.R. 228.

b. Materially altered the dominant tenement,[34] or

c. Acquiesced in an interference with the easement by the servient owner. The interference – "adverse possession" – may cause the extinguishment of the easement under the Statute of Limitations, 1957.

3. Merger

An easement will be extinguished if the dominant and servient tenements come into the ownership and possession of the same person. Unity of ownership here means acquisition of both tenements for a fee simple absolute.[35]

4. Statute

Easements may be extinguished, expressly or impliedly, by statute.

PROFITS À PRENDRE

A profit may be regarded as a type of easement. It is a right to use another's land by removing a portion of the land or its products. A profit, unlike an easement, may exist independently of a dominant tenement; this is commonly expressed by saying that a profit may exist in gross.

The common law profits are:– 1. Turbary – the right to remove turf for use as fuel; 2. Piscary – the right to fish; 3. Estovers – the right to cut timber for fuel; and 4. Pasture – the right to have animals graze.

Contemporary interests in land that are sometimes called profits are the right to mine coal or other minerals, or to drill for oil or coal, or to cut timber. Generally, a profit

---

34. See, e.g., *Moore* v. *Rawson* [1824] 3 B. & C. 32; and *Lloyd's Bank Ltd* v. *Dalton* [1942] 2 All E.R. 352.
35. See, e.g., *R.* v. *Inhabitants of Hermitage* [1692] Carth 239.

carries incidental easements with it; for instance, the right to mine coal carries the incidental right to enter into the mine.

A profit may be enjoyed by one person or by a group of people. Profits, as well as easements, must be distinguished from similar interests in property such as licences, public rights and the rights of fluctuating bodies.[36]

ACQUISITION OF PROFITS

1. Express Grant or Reservation

The relevant principles are the same as for easements. Thus, for instance, the grantee must be capable.[37]

2. Implied Grant or Reservation

Implied profits may be acquired only under the doctrine of intention.

3. Prescription

1. Common Law
The relevant principles are the same as for easements.[38]
2. Lost Modern Grant
The relevant principles are the same as for easements.[39]
3. Statutory
The relevant principles are the same as for easements except that:–

    a. The periods are thirty and sixty years, and
    b. One can make a statutory prescriptive claim only

---

36. See, e.g., *Radcliff* v. *Hayes* [1907] 1 I.R. 101.
37. See, e.g., *Westropp* v. *Congested Districts Bd.* [1919] 1 I.R. 224.
38. See, e.g., *Convey* v. *Regan* [1952] I.R. 56.
39. See, e.g., *Neaverson* v. *Peterborough R.D.C.* [1902] 1 Ch. 557.

for a profit appurtenent,i.e., the right claimed must be in respect of a dominant tenement.

EXTINGUISHMENT OF PROFITS

The relevant principles are the same as for easements.[40]

---

40. See, supra, at pages 95 and 96.

8

Succession

INTRODUCTION

Succession law concerns the distribution of property on a person's death. The general rule is that every person has freedom of testation, namely, the power to provide by will for the disposal of his property on death. Failure to exercise this power over all or part of a person's property results in an intestacy. The disposal of property on intestacy is governed by the Succession Act, 1965.[1]

The estate of a deceased person must be administered before distribution is made to those entitled on the testacy or intestacy. The administration is carried out by the personal representatives. The personal representatives first ascertain the assets and liabilities of the deceased. They must then obtain a grant of representation, which is an order of the court, and which confers upon them the authority to administer the estate of the deceased. The grant of representation takes the form of a grant of probate in the event of testacy, and of letters of administration in the event of intestacy. The personal representatives, acting under the grant of representation, may now realise at least sufficient of the assets as are necessary to pay all debts and liabilities properly payable. The balance, or net estate, can then be distributed among those beneficially entitled.

---

1. This Act operates in respect of all deaths occurring after January 1, 1967.

It is proposed to consider the following aspects of succession law in particular:– the beneficial devolution of realty and personalty on intestacy prior to the Succession Act; the beneficial devolution of all property on intestacy after the Succession Act; and various aspects of the law relating to wills.

A knowledge of the rules governing the succession to property before the Succession Act continues to be of importance. For instance, if one is acting for a purchaser of unregistered property, one must trace the title back a period of years – the normal minimum period is twenty years.

BENEFICIAL DEVOLUTION OF REALTY ON INTESTACY BEFORE THE SUCCESSION ACT

Inheritance of land before the Succession Act was determined in accordance with the doctrine of primogeniture and by the common law canons of descent, but subject to the right – namely, curtesy or dower – of the surviving spouse.

Apart from local custom, the primary doctrine of inheritance was primogeniture. The doctrine that inheritance was impartial – that a deceased had only one heir-at-law – was obviously congenial to the feudal system, since feudal relations were disturbed as little as possible.

The canons of descent provided for inheritance by any blood relative no matter how remote the relationship, and this is also true under the scheme in the Succession Act. This policy has, nevertheless, been the subject of criticism for many years, especially since it may work to cast the inheritance on a distant relative with whom the deceased had no personal or social ties, the "laughing heir" as he has been called.

It is sufficient at this point to note that the rights of the surviving spouse, to curtesy or dower, had early origins in English law.[2] For instance, under Magna Carta the widow had a right to "tarry in the chief house of her husband for forty days".

Ascertainment of Heir

Following are the rules whereby heirship on intestacy was determined prior to the Succession Act.

Trace from last Purchaser

Rule 1. The heir was traced from the last purchaser. The last purchaser was any person who acquired the land otherwise than by descent on intestacy, escheat, partition or inclosure. The person last entitled was deemed to be the last purchaser until the contrary was shown.

One qualification to this rule was that, if the last purchaser had no heir, descent could be traced from the person last entitled.

Issue

Rule 2. The issue were preferred to other relatives, the male issue being preferred to the female issue.

Rule 3. The elder male was preferred to the younger male, but females of the same degree took equally as co-parceners.

Rule 4. Issue of a deceased person represented him, being preferred among themselves according to rules 2 and 3.

Ancestors and Collaterals

Rule 5. If the last purchaser left no issue, his nearest lineal ancestor was entitled, issue of a deceased ancestor

---

2. Curtesy and dower are discussed, *infra*, at pages 102 and 103.

representing the ancestor according to rule 4.

Rule 6. Paternal ancestors and their issue were preferred to maternal ancestors and their issue, and male paternal ancestors and their issue were preferred to female paternal ancestors and their issue.

Rule 7. The mother of the more remote male paternal ancestor and her issue were preferred to the mother of the less remote male paternal ancestor and her issue.

Rule 8. On failure of paternal ancestors and their issue, similar rules applied to the maternal ancestors and their issue.

Relatives of the Half Blood

Two persons are said to be related by the half blood when they trace descent from different marriages of a common ancestor.

Rule 9. If the common ancestor was a male, relatives of the half blood took next after any relative of the same degree of the whole blood and his issue.

Rule 10. If the common ancestor was a female, relatives of the half blood took next after her.

Curtesy and Dower

The rights of the heir on intestacy were, as already stated, subject to curtesy or dower.

(a) Curtesy

This was the right of a widower to a life estate in the entire realty of his deceased wife.

The principal prerequisites to the existence of curtesy were as follows:–

1. only heritable freehold estates could be the subject of curtesy;
2. the deceased wife, prior to her death, had to be

seized or possessed of the land;

3. issue of the marriage capable of inheriting the land must have been born; and
4. the wife must not have disposed of the land either inter vivos or by will.

(b) Dower

This was the right of a widow to a life estate in one-third of the realty of her deceased husband.

The principal prerequisites to the existence of dower were as follows:–

1. only heritable freehold estates could be the subject of dower;
2. the deceased husband, prior to his death, had to be seized or possessed of the land;
3. issue of the marriage capable of inheriting the land must have been capable of being born; and
4. the husband must not have disposed of the land either inter vivos or by will, or must not have made a declaration under the Dower Act 1833 barring dower.

A widow could enjoy her right to dower either by having one-third of the land assigned to her for life, or by receiving one-third of the income from the land during her life.

DETERMINING DEGREES OF KINSHIP

The general policy of the law of intestate succession is that the nearest in blood to the deceased should benefit. The distance between relatives and a deceased for purpose of inheritance is measured in terms of degrees of kinship. A gloss on this policy is constituted by the principle of inheritance by representation that sometimes pertains.

Statutes governing intestacy usually provide for inheritance in a certain order, by designating groups, such as, brothers and sisters; in the absence of any member of one of these specifically designated groups, it is usually provided that the estate shall go to the next-of-kin or the next of kin in equal degree. Such provisions make it necessary to determine degrees of relationship between the deceased and those claiming a share of the estate. Such degrees of kinship must be counted up or down, and cannot be counted sideways.

Descendants and Ancestors

In its primary sense, one degree means a difference of one generation and, when a question arises as to the relationship of the intestate and one of his descendants, this primary meaning is controlling. A child of the intestate is one generation removed and is, therefore, in the first degree, a grandchild is in the second degree, and so forth. The same method of computing degrees is used for those in the ascending line.

Collaterals

The method used for determining the kinship of collaterals to a deceased goes back to the interpretation by the English judges of the Statute of Distributions of 1670:[3] this provided for distribution of personal property to the "next of kindred in equal degree" in the event of the deceased leaving no descendants. The English judges adopted the civil law method of computing degrees, which consists of counting generations from the intestate to the common ancestor, and then down from the common ancestor to the collateral relative who claims a share of the estate. This means, for instance, that an uncle is related in the third degree. The common ancestor of both will be the intestate's grandfather, who is two degrees removed counting upwards. The third degree is constituted by counting down from the grandfather to the uncle.

---

3.   This Act was applied to Ireland in 1695.

Inheritance by Representation

Taking by representation is usually referred to as taking per stirpes. The central idea in taking by representation – i.e., taking, not in one's own right, but in the right of an ancestor – is that a person is entitled to the share that his ancestor would have taken had he survived the intestate.

Where taking by representation is not permitted, those entitled on intestacy are referred to as taking per capita. This signifies that issue of a deceased person who, if he were alive, would be entitled on another's intestacy, are not permitted to stand in his shoes for purposes of succession.

BENEFICIAL DEVOLUTION OF PERSONALTY ON INTESTACY BEFORE THE SUCCESSION ACT

Intestate succession to personalty (and also leaseholds) before the Succession Act was not subject to the doctrine of primogeniture and the canons of descent that governed intestate succession to realty. The explanation is historical. Whereas the early common law courts had jurisdiction over succession to realty, the jurisdiction over succession to personalty in feudal times lay with the ecclesiastical courts. The following extract from Holdsworth explains the situation:–

> "The ecclesiastical courts obtained jurisdiction over grants of Probate and Administration, and, to a certain degree, over the conduct of the executor and the administrator. All these branches of their jurisdiction could be exercised only over personal estate. This abandonment of jurisdiction to the ecclesiastical courts has tended, more than any other single cause, to accentuate the difference between real and personal property; for even when the ecclesiastical courts had

ceased to exercise some parts of this jurisdiction, the law which they had created was exercised by their successors."[4]

The principal objective of the Statute of Distributions[5] in the seventeenth century was to strengthen the power of the ecclesiastical courts over the administration of personal estate. It failed in this objective – chancery courts subsequently supplanted the ecclesiastical courts in this branch of the law. The statute, nevertheless, has had resounding effect. Its provisions for distribution of personal estate on intestacy applied with only slight variations until 1967.[6] Moreover, these distributive provisions have shaped the modern law of intestate succession, including that contained in the Succession Act governing both real and personal estate.

Rules for Ascertaining the Next-of-Kin Who Should Benefit

The general principle was that an intestate's personalty, including leaseholds, passed to the next-of-kin of the same degree in equal shares, and these took as tenants in common.

The idea of tracing from the last purchaser did not arise. The following were the principal rules:-

Rule 1. Where a wife died intestate leaving a surviving husband and (possibly) issue, the husband took the

---

4. I Holdsworth, *History of English Law,* (7th. ed. 1965), p. 625.
5. The statute was passed in England in 1670, and adapted to Ireland in 1695.
6. The principal variations on the distributive provisions of the Statute of Distributions, as these had applied to the intestate succession to personal estate in respect of deaths occuring before 1967, derived from the Intestate Estates Acts, 1890 and 1954, and from the doctrine of advancement.

entire personalty to the exclusion of other relatives.

Rule 2. Where a husband died intestate leaving a surviving wife and issue, the wife took one-third and the issue took two-thirds per stirpes.

Rule 3. Where a husband died intestate leaving a surviving wife and no issue, the wife took half and the nearest next-of-kin took the other half.[7]

Rule 4. The issue of a deceased person (including any issue en ventre sa mère) took per stirpes, males taking equally with females and the younger equally with the elder.

Rule 5. If neither spouse nor issue were surviving, and the father of the deceased was surviving, he took absolutely.

Rule 6. If neither spouse, issue nor father were surviving, but a mother, and either brothers or sisters were surviving, these shared equally. Children, but not remoter descendants, of a deceased brother or sister took their parent's share.

Rule 7. If neither spouse, issue nor parents were surviving, but brothers and sisters and either nephews or nieces were surviving, these took equally, the nephews and nieces taking per stirpes.

Rule 8. If neither spouse, issue, parents nor brothers and sisters were surviving, the personalty was divisible per capita between the next-of-kin of the same degree.

Rule 9. Relatives of the half blood took equally with relatives of the whole blood, i.e., there was no preference for relatives of the whole blood.

---

7. This rule was qualified by the Intestates Estate Act, 1954, this Act having replaced the Intestates Estate Act, 1890. See, infra, at pages 108 and 109.

ADVANCEMENTS

Advancements to children have been subject to the hotchpot rule under both the pre- and post-Succession Act law.

The rule, in short, is that any advancement made to a child of a deceased person, prior to the date of death, must be taken into account as between the children in calculating the share of the child who received the advancement.

An advancement denotes any payment to a child that is designed to finance a more than temporary betterment of the child. The payment will normally be by way of a capital sum.

The rule relating to advancements and hotchpot is retained in section 63 of the Succession Act. Following, however, are differences between the rule in its present form and in its form prior to the Succession Act:–

1. The existing rule applies to both realty and personalty; it applied only to personalty before the Succession Act;

2. The existing rule applies on the intestacy of either a father or mother; it applied only on the intestacy of a father before the Succession Act; and

3. The existing rule applies on a partial intestacy as well as on a complete intestacy; it applied only on a complete intestacy before the Succession Act.

INTESTATES' ESTATE ACTS, 1890 and 1954

These Acts made certain qualifications to the rules already noted as to the beneficial devolution of both realty and personalty on intestacy prior to the Succession Act. Under the Intestates' Estate Act, 1890, where a person died

leaving a wife but no issue, the wife was entitled to every-
thing absolutely if the realty and personalty did not exceed
£500.00; if the value did exceed £500.00, the wife was entitled
to a first charge of £500.00.[8]

The 1890 Act was replaced by the Intestates Estate Act,
1954, which substituted the figure of £4,000.00 for the
£500.00 previously provided for.[9]

The right given to a surviving wife by these Acts was
in addition to any right of dower she might have, and also
in addition to her distributive share of the personalty.

BENEFICIAL DEVOLUTION OF ALL PROPERTY
ON INTESTACY AFTER THE SUCCESSION ACT

Introduction

The Succession Act ended the bifurcated system for
succession on intestacy. It introduced new rules governing
the intestate succession to all property, real and personal,
in respect of deaths occurring after January 1, 1967. These
rules were largely inspired by the pre-Succession Act provisions governing intestate succession to personal estate.
Moreover, "[The] rules are simple, uniform and so framed
as to accord due recognition to the important position which
the wife occupies in the Irish family".[10]

Before considering sections 66 to 73 of the Succession
Act, it can be noted that:- first, curtesy and dower have
been abolished, by section 11 of the Succession Act, 1965;
secondly, the Intestates' Estates Act, 1954, and the
Administration of Estates Act, 1959, have been repealed;
and thirdly, the doctrine of advancement now has a statutory basis, in section 63 of the Succession Act, 1965.

---

8. Intestates' Estates Act, 1890, s. 1.
9. Intestates' Estate Act, 1954, ss. 3 to 5.
10. Parliamentary Debates: Official Report, Vol. 213, No. 3.

Rules for Distribution of All Property on Intestacy After the Succession Act

Following is an account of the rules in tabular form. Those lower in the table take only in the absence of those higher up. Another preliminary point is that, under section 66, it is the "net estate" that is available for distribution.

RELATIVE(S) SURVIVING	SHARE
Section 67	
Spouse Only	All.
Spouse and Issue	Spouse takes two-thirds and issue take remainder in accordance with sub-section 4.
Issue Only	Issue take all in accordance with sub-section 4.
Section 68:	
Parents	Each takes one-half as tenants in common.
Parent	All.
Section 69:	
Brothers and Sisters and their children	They take as tenants in common. Children of a deceased brother or sister take their parent's share.
Nephews and Nieces	They take as tenants in common.
Section 70:	
Next of kin	These take as tenants in common in accordance with section 71. Taking by representation is admitted only in the case of children of brothers and sisters of the intestate where any brother or sister of the intestate survives him.

Section 71

"Next-of-kin" means the person(s) standing nearest in blood relationship to the deceased at the date of death.

Degrees of kinship are counted in the manner already discussed. The section, however, introduced one innovation in the method of computation, i.e.,

> "where a direct lineal ancestor and any other relative are so ascertained to be within the same degree of blood relationship to the intestate, the other relative shall be preferred to the exclusion of the direct lineal ancestor."[11]

Thus, for instance, an uncle would take to the exclusion of the great-grandfather of an intestate.

Section 72

Relatives of the half-blood take equally with relatives of the whole blood in the same degree. This is new as regards real estate.

Section 73

In default of next-of-kin, the estate of an intestate passes to the State as ultimate intestate successor. This provision replaces the pre-Succession Act rules of forfeiture by escheat in the case of realty, and of bona vacantia in the case of personalty.

VARIOUS ASPECTS OF THE LAW RELATING TO WILLS

Introduction

A will may be defined as "a declaration in prescribed form of the person making it of the matters which he wishes to take effect on or after his death, until which time it is

---

11. Succession Act, 1965, s. 71(2).

revocable". The term will also includes a codicil.[12]

Although the will has predominance as an instrument for disposing of property on death, the same objective may be attained by an inter vivos settlement. The donatia mortis causa provides another alternative to the will; this concept however has limited application.

The modern will derives from Roman origin. Adapted by the Normans into English law, its recognition as a dispositive instrument was limited during feudal times because of the opposition of the common law courts to the power of testation. The early restrictions on this power were circumvented by deployment of the use concept to dispose of property on death. Then came the Statute of Uses, 1535:—[13]

> "[The] Statute was intended to abolish the power to devise land and was generally believed to have done so. In fact, it increased the power of testators by making it possible for them to devise legal estates instead of mere equitable interests, by means of executed uses. This, however, was not realised at the time, and the supposed abolition of the power to devise was so unpopular that it became one of the causes of rebellion known as the Pilgrimage of Grace, 1536. As a concession the Statute of Wills was passed in 1540."[14]

That statute, as amended, regulated wills until the Wills Act, 1837,[15] was passed. The Wills Act, as amended, was in turn repealed and replaced by the Succession Act, 1965.

---

12. Succession Act, 1965, s. 3.
13. 27 Hen. 8, c. 100.
14. Megarry and Wade, *The Law of Real Property* (3rd. ed., 1966), p. 167.
15. 7 Will. 481 Vict. c. 26.

Essentials of the Validity of Wills

1. Testator's Capacity

A capable testator is one who:– (a) has attained eighteen years or is, or has been, married, and (b) is of sound disposing mind.[16]

2. Animus Testandi

Animus Testandi refers to the mental state of the testator. It means that he must:– first, understand what he is doing, i.e., making a will, secondly, be free of vitiating mental disorder, and thirdly, exercise his genuine free choice in making the will.

3. Compliance with Statutory Formalities

The formalities prescribed for wills are set out in section 78 of the Succession Act, 1965. The most important of these are as follows:

1. a will must be in writing;
2. it must be signed by the testator or by some person in his presence and by his direction at the foot of the will;
3. the testator's signature must be made or acknowledged in the presence of two witnessess, present together; and
4. both witnesses must sign their names in the testator's presence.

It may be noted that it is not necessary that the witnesses sign in the presence of each other. Also, although it is normal practice to include an attestation clause on behalf of

---

16. Succession Act, 1965, s. 77.

the witnesses, such a clause is not mandatory.

Revocation of Wills

A will is revocable until death, provided that the testator has full mental capacity. This principle applies, notwithstanding that a will when made was accompanied by an agreement not to revoke – breach of such an agreement may give rise to an action in damages, but any revocation will be effective.

A will can only be revoked in the following ways:–

1. By Marriage

"A will shall be revoked by the subsequent marriage of the testator, except a will made in contemplation of that marriage, whether so expressed in the will or not."[17]

2. By a Document

A will may be revoked by "[Another] will or codicil duly executed, or by some writing declaring an intention to revoke it and executed in the manner in which a will is required to be executed. . ."[18]

Express revocation clauses are common in wills. Moreover, there is a general rule of construction that where there are inconsistent testamentary instruments, the later instrument revokes the earlier to the extent of the inconsistency.

3. By Actual Destruction

A will may be revoked by "[The] burning, tearing, or destruction of it by the testator, or by some person in his

---

17. Succession Act, 1965, s. 85(1).
18. Succession Act, 1965, s. 85(2).

presence and by his direction, with the intention of revoking it".[19]

Although symbolic destruction is not sufficient, it is not necessary to mutilate a will so that it is rendered entirely illegible. The act of destruction required to revoke a will must be done with animus revocandi:– "All the destroying in the world without intention will not revoke a will, nor will all the intention in the world without destroying. There must be the two."[20]

Revival of Wills

Revival is the restoration to effect of a will or codicil that has been revoked. A will may be revived only by re-execution or by a subsequent codicil.[21] To show a revival, it is necessary that there be:– first, a formal act of revival; secondly, an intention to revive; and thirdly, the existence of the will.

POWER OF TESTATION

Testamentary power over personal estate has been recognised from very remote times. It appears however that the Normans introduced some restrictions on the power of testation over personal estate. Thus, there was recognition of the "wife's part", the "bairn's part" and the "dead's part". These restrictions disappeared in the fourteenth century.

Testamentary power over real estate emerged only in the sixteenth century. It had been restricted until that time by the common law courts, which viewed the power as being inconsistent with the concepts and policies of feudalism.

---

19. Succession Act, 1965, s. 85(2).
20. Per James, L.J., in *Cheese* v. *Lovejoy* [1877] 2 P.D. 251.
21. Succession Act, 1965, s. 87.

Freedom of testation, as already noted, was available in respect of personal and real estate from the fourteenth and sixteenth centuries, respectively, onwards. This freedom was subject only to certain regulations designed to minimise the possibility of perjury and forgery, so that the nearest relative could still be excluded from succession without even the proverbial shilling.

It remains the general rule that dispositions of a testator will be given effect to in accordance with the terms of the will. Important qualifications to this rule, however, are now provided for in the Succession Act. These qualifications, apart from those contained in sections 63 and 82, were new to Irish succession law in respect of deaths arising after 1967. The principal qualifications are as follows:–

1. *Right of Surviving Spouse to Appropriation of Dwelling and Household Chattels*

The Succession Act confers on a surviving spouse the right to require that the dwelling and household chattels be appropriated in satisfaction, in whole or in part, of any share to which he or she becomes entitled on the death, testate or intestate, of the deceased spouse.[22] A surviving spouse, in order to exercise the right, must serve the prescribed notice on the personal representatives requiring them to make the appropriation.

2. *Advancements to be Taken into Account*

The doctrine of advancement, as already noted, has a statutory basis in section 63 of the Succession Act. The doctrine requires that, in calculating the respective shares of children on a parent's death (testate or intestate), account be taken of any advancement made to the child during the

---

22. Succession Act, 1965, s. 56.

lifetime of the deceased parent.
An advancement denotes:

> "[A] gift intended to make permanent provision for a child, and includes advancement by way of portion or settlement, including any life or lesser interest and including property covenanted to be paid or settled. It also includes an advancement or portion for the purpose of establishing a child in a profession, vocation, trade or business, a marriage portion and payments made for the education of a child to a standard higher than that provided by the deceased for any other or others of his children."[23]

The doctrine applies under the Act, but "[Subject] to any contrary intention expressed or appearing from the circumstances of the case".

3. Gifts to an Attesting Witness, or to the Spouse of Such a Witness, are Void.

A witness to a will, or his spouse, may not benefit under the will.[24] This type of provision has long been a feature in statutes governing wills. The object of the provision is to obviate fraud and other vitiating factors in the drawing of wills; this, it is believed, can be achieved by an insistence on disinterested witnesses.

An exception is made in the section in relation to "[Charges] and directions for the payment of any debt or debts".[25] Thus, for instance, where a solicitor who attests a will is also appointed executor, an express provision in the will entitling him to charge for his services will be valid.

---

23. Succession Act, 1965, s. 63(6).
24. Succession Act, 1965, s. 82.
25. Succession Act, 1965, s. 83.

It can be noted that a gift to an attesting witness or his spouse does not invalidate a will – only the gift itself is void.

4. "Forced Share" Provisions

The power of testation, as it had developed prior to the Succession Act, was unfettered, so that even a surviving spouse might be left destitute. The so-called marital estates, i.e., curtesy and dower, represented the only protection of a surviving spouse against disinheritance by the terms of a will. The protection afforded by these estates was, however, largely illusory. The estates were easily barred. Moreover, personal estate has formed an ever-increasing proportion of wealth since the nineteenth century, and only real estate was within the catchment of marital estates.

The forced share provisions of the Succession Act now afford adequate protection to a surviving spouse.[26] These provisions assure a legal right share to a surviving spouse. The share is one-half of the estate if the testator leaves a spouse and no children. The share is one third of the estate if the testator leaves a spouse and also children. It can be noted that the legal right share is equivalent to half of what a surviving spouse would take on an intestacy.

A spouse may renounce his entitlement to a legal right share by contract.[27]

Also, where a testator, during his lifetime, has made permanent provision for his spouse, this provision shall be taken as having been given in or towards satisfaction of the legal right share of the spouse.

A devise or bequest in a will that is expressed to be in addition to the legal right share of a spouse takes effect as such. In any other case, such a devise or bequest shall be deemed to have been intended in satisfaction of the legal

---

26. Succession Act, 1965, ss. 111 to 116.
27. Succession Act, 1965, s. 113.

right share of the spouse.[28]

A surviving spouse may be obliged to elect between a legal right share and other entitlements. Consider, first, where a deceased spouse dies wholly testate – here the election will be between any testamentary benefits and the legal right share. Consider, secondly, where the deceased spouse dies partly testate – here the election will be between any testamentary benefits together with the share on intestacy on the one hand, and the legal right share on the other hand. A surviving spouse, if he fails to make a timely election, forfeits his legal right share.[29]

5. Provision for Children

Children are not entitled to a forced share under the Succession Act. Application may however be made to the court by, or on behalf of, a child who has been disinherited or inadequately provided for by the will of his parents.[30]

The court, on foot of such application, has a discretionary power to order such provision to be made for the child as it considers just. The court must consider the application from "the point of view of a prudent and just parent".

---

28. Succession Act, 1965, s. 114.
29. Succession Act, 1965, s. 115.
30. Succession Act, 1965, s. 117.

Part Two

Conveyancing Law

Summary of Part Two

  9. Stages in a Conveyance   123
10. The Contract of Sale   128
11. The Standard Contract of Sale   139
12. Title to be Shown under an Open Contract   155
13. Consents Required under the Land Act, 1965   161
14. Form and Effect of a Conveyance of a Fee Simple 169
15. Agency and Conveyancing   183

9

Stages in a Conveyance

INTRODUCTION

Conveyancing is commonly regarded as one of the more practical branches of law. It is moreover one of considerable complexity, and one in which the risk factor is normally high because of, among other reasons, the high value placed on real property.

Prior to considering the general principles of conveyancing law, it is proposed to outline the standard practice in a typical conveyancing transaction of unregistered property in order to provide the context for the subsequent consideration of the relevant principles.

FIRST STAGE: FROM PRELIMINARY NEGOTIATIONS TO CONTRACT

The solicitor for the vendor, having been instructed to act, will acquire the title documents to the property and will draw up the contract of sale. The contract is normally drawn in the current form of the standard particulars and conditions of sale made available by the Incorporated Law Society of Ireland. The contract in duplicate, together with the documents of title listed in the documents schedule of the standard contract, are then forwarded to the solicitor for the purchaser.

The latter, in consultation with his client, will examine

the contract with a view to possible amendments, and will also conduct an initial examination of the title that is being offered. Other preliminary issues will also be attended to; for instance, planning searches may be made, the financing of the purchase will be reviewed and also further enquiries relating to the title may be addressed to the vendor's solicitor. Eventually, the contract of sale in duplicate, possibly with amendments, will be signed by the purchaser, and returned to the vendor's solicitor together with the deposit.

If still prepared to proceed with the sale after further consultation with his solicitor, the vendor will sign the contract of sale in duplicate. One copy of the executed contract, together with the remainder of the copy title documents, are then forwarded to the purchaser's solicitor.[1]

SECOND STAGE: FROM CONTRACT TO CLOSING

The solicitor for the purchaser may now commence the formal investigation of title. This examination will take a number of forms, including the following. The title documents are examined with a view to tracing the title from a good root of title. Also, the formal requisitions on title are forwarded to the vendor's solicitor, possibly with a draft deed for approval. In addition, relevant searches are made in the Registry of Deeds. Subsidiary searches should also be made where appropriate. These may include:– searches in the Bankruptcy Office, in the Lis Pendens Register, in the Judgements Register, in the Local Planning Office, in

---

1. Numerous variations on the foregoing typical procedure at the first stage of a conveyancing transaction may apply. For instance, the preliminary enquiries will obviously be more extensive where the property involved is an apartment in a new condominium, or a licensed premises, than where the property involved is an existing residence. Moreover, occasionally, and particularly in the context of large sales, the contract may be concluded by the exchange of contracts method.

the Sheriff's Office, in the Companies Office, in the Register of Friendly Societies, and in the District Court Office.

The solicitor for the vendor, in consultation with his client, will reply to the requisitions on title and will return one copy to the purchaser's solicitor together with the draft deed as approved. The latter, if satisfied with the replies to the requisitions, will then engross the draft deed and prepare a memorial of it. The engrossment, the memorial and the draft deed will then be forwarded to the vendor's solicitor, who will arrange for the execution of the deed and memorial by the vendor. The vendor's solicitor at this point may forward an apportionment account, together with relevant vouchers and receipts, to the solicitor for the purchaser.

The latter, if satisfied with the title and with the results of the examinations of other matters relating to the transaction, will then arrange an appointment to close the sale. He will request the purchaser to furnish the balance due on closing, and also the amount necessary to cover stamp duty and costs. A bank draft for the sum due on closing is then prepared. At this time, also, the purchaser may be advised to arrange permanent insurance on the property as and from the appointed closing date.[2]

---

2. The following are some of the possible variations on the typical procedure at the second stage of a conveyancing transaction noted above. First, where the property is registered, a draft transfer takes the place of the draft deed, and there will be no need of a memorial. Also, instead of a search in the Registry of Deeds, an official or priority search will be made in the Land Registry. Secondly, a number of additional items will require to be attended to by a solicitor for the purchaser where the purchase is being financed by a loan. For instance, title will require to be certified to the bank from which the purchaser is obtaining any bridging accommodation, and also undertakings will be furnished relating to the disposal of the mortgage loan. In addition, the purchaser's solicitor may correspond with the financial institution from which the purchaser has obtained long term loan sanction.

THIRD STAGE: CLOSING

The closing of the sale normally occurs at the office of the vendor's solicitor. The latter will produce the original title documents, the evidence necessary to discharge the requisitions, and also the conveyance and the memorial executed by the vendor. These documents, together with any undertakings required by the solicitor for the purchaser, are exchanged for the balance of the purchase money.[3]

FOURTH STAGE: AFTER CLOSING

Several matters will normally remain to be attended by the solicitor for the vendor after the sale has been closed. A closing account, a copy of the apportionment account, a fee note and the balance of the proceeds of sale may be sent to the vendor. The latter is also advised to cancel any insurances on the property that has been conveyed. In addition, if he has not already done so, the vendor's solicitor will notify the relevant rates department of the change of ownership, and also notify the lessor of the property of the assignment if the title of the property sold was leasehold.

A number of important matters will also remain for the attention of the purchaser's solicitor. The deed of conveyance and memorial will require to be stamped and

---

3. Several variations on the typical procedure at the third stage of a conveyancing transaction are again possible. For instance, if the property is registered, the deed of conveyance will take the form of a Land Registry transfer. The essential document of title will be a land certificate, and other documents peculiar to the Registration of Title system – for instance, a Land Registry map and a section 72 declaration may be required.

registered and relevant accounts will be furnished to the purchaser.[4]

---

4. As with the other stages, the above typical procedure at the stage of a conveyance after a sale has been closed is subject to numerous variations of which the following are illustrations. First, if the property is registered, the Land Registry transfer will require to be registered in the Land Registry in order to establish the purchaser's title. Secondly, if the purchaser is availing of a mortgage, a procedure similar to that which took place between vendor and purchaser will be adopted between the purchaser and the mortgagee. Thirdly, if the vendor had closed the sale on the basis of an undertaking to the purchaser to discharge any encumbrance on the property sold out of the proceeds of sale, this undertaking will require to be satisfied.

10

The Contract of Sale

TYPES OF CONTRACT

Three types of contract of sale can be distinguished, namely, verbal, formal written, and open and written contracts. All such contracts are valid but, in general, only the latter two types are enforceable by reason of the requirements of the Statute of Frauds.[1] The usual features of these contracts, and also the statutory requirements, will now be considered.

1. Verbal Contract

The term verbal contract needs no explanation. Notwithstanding that the parties have agreed verbally on the property, the price and the other provisions of the sale, the general rule is that verbal contracts are unenforceable.

2. Formal Written Contract

This is the most common type of contract in practice. It is normally drawn in the standard form issued by the Incorporated Law Society of Ireland. It will provide for the parties, the property, the price and also the other provisions of the sale.[2] The standard form contract currently in use was issued in 1988. It virtually reproduces the 1986 edition, apart from a few amendments.

---

1. Statute of Frauds (Ireland) Act, 1695.
2. See, infra, Chapter 11 at page 139 et seq.

3. *Open and Written Contract*

The parties to a sale may draft their own written contract providing for the essentials of the transaction. This approach is extremely inadvisable, and is in fact rare. Nevertheless, a contract so prepared will be enforceable if it complies with the Statute of Frauds.

COMPLIANCE OF CONTRACT OF SALE WITH STATUTE OF FRAUDS

A contract for the sale of an interest in land – apart from complying with the three essentials of a valid contract – must comply with the formalities prescribed in section 2 of the Statute of Frauds (Ireland) Act, 1695:–

> "No action shall be brought by any person upon any contract of sale of lands unless the agreement upon which such action shall be brought or some memorandum or note thereof shall be in writing and signed by the party to be charged therewith or some other person lawfully authorised to sign."

Analysis of the Requirements

(1) *Written Agreement or Memorandum thereof in Writing*

The written agreement or memorandum must, at a minimum, describe the parties, the property, the price and any other provisions agreed by the parties. The descriptions must be such as to provide adequate identification. Illustratively, a signature, or a description of one party as owner where the property is identified, would be sufficient as a description of the vendor.

The writing will normally be in the form of a contract of sale. However, other forms of writing have been held to suffice. These include an initialled rent book, a receipt for a deposit and mere letters. Moreover, an adequate memorandum may be constituted by several documents.[3]

(2) Signature of Party to be Charged or of his Authorised Agent

Only the party to be charged under the contract need have signed it. The phrase "agent thereto lawfully authorised" is to be interpreted according to general agency principles. Thus, the signature of one person will bind another person if it was made under express, implied or apparent authority, or if the signature, although originally unauthorised, was later ratified.[4] The question of whether a person becomes a party to a contract for the sale of an interest in land by virtue of the signature of an agent arises principally where the agent is either a solicitor or an auctioneer.

A solicitor has no implied or ostensible authority to sign a contract of sale for his client arising from the solicitor-client relationship. Thus, a solicitor's signature will make his client a party to a contract only if the signature was expressly or apparently authorised or subsequently ratified.[5]

In the absence of special circumstances, by virtue of his employment, an auctioneer is impliedly the agent of both the vendor and the purchaser to sign the contract or a note or memorandum thereof to satisfy the Statute of Frauds. This implied authority cannot be revoked, after the conclusion of the bidding, either by the vendor or the purchaser. It must, however, be exercised at the time of

---

3. See, e.g., *Timmins* v. *Moreland Street Property Company Ltd.* [1958] Ch. 110.
4. See, e.g., *Brennan* v. *O'Connell and Another* [1975] Unrep. [Sup. Ct., I.R.] [1974 No. 8].
5. See, e.g., *Cloncurry* v. *Laffan* [1924] I.R. 78.

the sale or while the transaction of sale is still in being, and an auctioneer has no authority to sign on a subsequent day or in a sale otherwise than by auction.[6] An estate agent, as such, has no authority to conclude a contract of sale.[7]

(3) Consequences where a Contract of Sale does not comply with the Statute of Frauds

Such a contract is valid but unenforceable by action. Either party can assert rights arising from such a contract insofar as these rights do not need to be enforced by action. The general rule is subject to certain qualifications. First, a verbal contract may be enforceable under the doctrine of part performance. Secondly, a verbal contract may be enforced if the defendant fails to plead the Statute. Thirdly, a party may waive the absence of the statutory requirements. Fourthly, a party can enforce a verbal contract where the failure to ensure compliance with the statutory requirements resulted from the fraud of the other party.

RELATIONSHIP ARISING BETWEEN VENDOR AND PURCHASER UNDER THE CONTRACT OF SALE

The position of the parties under a contract of sale, pending completion of the sale, is governed by principles of common law and equity, but subject to the express provisions of the contract. It is proposed here to outline the relevant principles at common law and equity, in terms of the rights and duties of the parties and also of their respective remedies for breach of contract.

---

6. See, e.g., *Phillips* v. *Butler* [1945] 2 All E.R. 285.
7. See, e.g., *Law* v. *Roberts and Co. (Ireland) Ltd.* [1964] I.R. 292.

Rights and Duties of the Purchaser

The purchaser becomes owner of the property in equity, and acquires what is referred to as an estate contract.[8] Moreover, the risk of loss to the property passes to the purchaser, and he acquires an insurable interest.[9] In addition, the purchaser becomes entitled to incidental benefits that accrue to the property prior to completion.

The purchaser is entitled to demand the title to the property, either as stipulated in the contract or as implied at law, and is also entitled to possession of the property on completion. Furthermore, if the vendor makes or permits a material alteration to the property prior to completion, the purchaser may be entitled either to damages for breach of contract or to rescission.[10]

The general principle is that the purchaser may assign the benefit of the contract. He can, moreover, waive provisions in the contract that are for his exclusive benefit.

Rights and Duties of the Vendor

A contract of sale creates the relationship of trustee and beneficiary between the vendor and purchaser. The vendor, consequently, has both a right and a duty to protect the property against third parties. He is moreover entitled to the rents and profits that issue from the property until completion of the sale. Conversely, the vendor is liable for all expenses properly attributable to the property during his period of beneficial enjoyment.

The vendor may allow a purchaser into possession prior to completion. This will usually be under a caretaker's

---

8.   See, e.g., *Tempany* v. *Hynes* [1976] I.R. 101.
9.   The common law position as to the passing of risk is modified in General Conditions 43 to 45 of the 1988 revised standard Contract of Sale issued by the Incorporated Law Society of Ireland. See, infra, Chapter 11 at page 153.
10.   See, e.g., *Bank of Ireland* v. *Waldrow* [1944] I.R. 303.

agreement that may regulate the relationship between the parties pending completion.

A vendor is entitled to the balance of the purchase money on completion of the sale, and can exercise a lien on the land in respect of this right.[11]

A vendor, in the same way as a purchaser, may waive provisions in the contract that are for his exclusive benefit.

Rights in the Nature of Remedies of Both Parties

The principal remedies available to either party for breach of a contract of sale by the other party include the following:– damages, rescission, specific performance, injunction and a declaration under a Vendor and Purchaser Summons. These remedies will be considered in turn.

1. Damages

An action for damages constitutes the basic remedy for breach of contract. However, it is not the most sought after remedy in relation to sales of land. Where the remedy is relevant, the measure of damages is calculated in accordance with general contractual principles.[12]

By way of a qualification on the general principles relating to the measure of damages, there may be applied "an anomalous rule based upon and justified by difficulties in showing a good title to real property in this country".[13] The rule referred to applies where the vendor is in breach of his duty to show good title. The purchaser in such case may recover only nominal damages for his loss of bargain – he would in addition recover any deposit paid, together with the conveyancing costs incurred.

---

11. See, e.g., *Munster and Leinster Bank Ltd.* v. *McGlashan* [1937] I.R. 525.
12. See, e.g., *Murphy* v. *Quality Homes* [1976] Unrep. [H.C., R.I.) [1975 No. 4344P].
13. Per Sargant J., in *Re Daniel, Daniel* v. *Vassall* [1971] 2 Ch. 405.

2. Rescission

Rescission is the most sought after remedy for breach of contract by vendors as a class. Rescission – a condition of which is complete restitution – may be available:– first, for breach of contract; secondly, for misrepresentation; thirdly, for mistake; or fourthly, in accordance with the contract.[14]

3. Specific Performance

Specific performance is the most sought after remedy for breach of contract by purchasers as a class. As an equitable remedy, it is granted only where damages would not afford adequate compensation.[15]

However, since the subject matter of every contract for the sale of land is regarded in Equity as unique, specific performance of such contracts is normally awarded almost as of right to purchasers. Vendors, likewise, are allowed the remedy almost as a matter of course – this result is prompted by a desire to achieve mutuality.

4. Injunction

The injunctive remedy is available with respect to contracts for the sale of land in accordance with general equitable remedies. It is particularly useful as a means of preventing breaches of contract.

5. Declaration

Many minor disputes between vendor and purchaser may be resolved by a declaration obtained by way of a vendor and purchaser summons. The procedure, which was introduced by section 9 of the Vendor and Purchaser Act, 1874, has been described as "a simple and inexpensive

---

14. See, e.g., *Harris* v. *Swordy* [1975] Unrep. [H.C., R.I.].
15. See, e.g., *White* v. *McCooey* [1976] Unrep. [H.C., R.I.].

method of settling disputes between vendor and purchaser".[16]

DISCHARGE OF THE CONTRACT

A contract for the sale of land is discharged on completion. Completion means "the complete conveyance of the estate and final settlement of the business".[17] The general rule is that after completion no action can be brought on the contract for sale:–

> "It is well settled that, where parties enter into an executory agreement which is to be carried out by a deed afterwards to be executed, the real completed contract is to be found in the deed."[18]

In consequence, for instance, the purchaser may no longer rely on the contractual stipulations as to title but must look instead to the covenants for title provided for in the deed.[19]

ENFORCEMENT OF THE CONTRACT OF SALE

Difficulties frequently occur regarding the enforcement of contracts for the sale of land. They usually arise simply because one party to the transaction has had second

---

16. Emmet on Title, 14th ed., Vol. 1., at 121.
17. Per Stable J., in *Killner* v. *France* [1946] 2 All E.R. 83.
18. See *Knight Sugar Co. Ltd.* v. *Alberta Railway & Irrigation Co.* [1938] 1 All E.R. 266.
19. The doctrine of merger is modified in General Condition 48 of the 1988 revised Standard Contract of Sale issued by the Incorporated Law Society of Ireland. See, infra, Chapter 11 at page 153.

thoughts on the sale. A vendor, for instance, may only after reflection realize the full implications of parting with his property, or he may decide to hold out for better terms. A purchaser, on the other hand, may conclude that his loan repayments arising on the purchase would be too onerous, or he may wish to wait until a property that would more fully meet his requirements becomes available.

At a certain point, however, the time for procrastination will, at law, be deemed to have passed. Both parties must then fulfil their promises or, alternatively, leave it open to the other party to pursue his remedies for non-performance.

The following catechism covers most situations in which a question arises as to whether an enforceable contract for sale exists:– first, is there a contract?; secondly, has the transaction been reduced to writing, signed by the party or his agent to be charged?; thirdly, is the writing sufficiently detailed?; and fourthly, is the contract free from suspensive conditions? If these questions can be answered affirmatively, an immediately enforceable contract will usually exist.

Some of the more usual issues raised by these questions will now be considered.

1. Contract distinguished from Agreement to Contract

A transaction that appears to constitute a contract of sale may be no more than an "agreement to agree".[20] If a transaction is of the latter type, it is not enforceable as a contract for the sale of land. It may be remarked that most conveyancers, at the stage when an attempt is being made to negotiate a sale, expressly stipulate that no binding transaction is to arise from the correspondence.

---

20. See, e.g., *Tiverton Estates Ltd.* v. *Wearwell Ltd.* [1974] 1 All E.R. 209; and *Kelly* v. *Park Hall School* [1979] I.R. 340. Since the cases referred to, the distinction between inchoate and concluded contracts of sale continues to be a fertile source of litigation that turns in large part on the particular circumstances of individual cases.

2. The Requirement of Writing

The requirement of writing has already been referred to. It is worth emphasizing that the contract itself need not be in writing provided that a memorandum of it exists.

Also, it may be stressed that the writing must be signed by "the party to be charged" or his agent. One may consider the situation where a purchaser gives a cheque by way of deposit on a sale, and the cheque is the only writing that has been executed; the vendor here, but not the purchaser, could enforce the contract.

3. Sufficiency of the Written Details

The writing, whether contained in a contract or a memorandum of a contract, must record all the essential terms that have been agreed. To express it another way, the writing must set out the parties, the property, the price and any other essential provisions that have been agreed, i.e., the "four P's"; otherwise the contract will be unenforceable.

The sufficiency of the writing as a record of the essential terms generally involves only questions of fact. It occasionally however involves questions of both law and fact. The issue in one case for instance was the sufficiency, for purposes of the Statute of Frauds, of a memorandum for the sale of a leasehold interest in certain building land. It was held that such a memorandum must, as a matter of law, state or indicate the date of commencement of the lease. The memorandum in question was insufficient on that basis.[21]

Only essential terms need be included in the writing. It has been held that a term is essential if it is regarded by

---

21. See, e.g., *O'Flaherty* v. *Arvan Properties Ltd.* [1977] Unrep. [Sup. Ct., R.I.].

the parties, or by one of them, as important – the test is subjective.[22]

4. Suspensive Conditions

A contract, although binding, may be unenforceable if it is subject to conditions precedent that remain unfulfilled. A party who has made a conditional contract must however make a bona fide effort to satisfy the condition(s).[23]

Another issue that has arisen in this regard is whether a purchaser can waive a condition in the contract, and proceed to enforcement. It has been held that this is permissible, provided that the condition is for the purchaser's own benefit.[24]

---

22. See, e.g., *Doherty* v. *Gallagher* [1975] Unrep. [H.C., R.I.] [1973 No. 2830 P].
23. *Costelloe* v. *Maharaj Krishna Properties (Ireland) Ltd.* [1975] Unrep. [H.C., R.I.] [1974 No. 1564 P] is on point. The purchaser there had contracted to purchase a stud farm. The agreement was subject to consent being obtained under the Land Act, 1965, s. 45. Application for the consent was made in a manner that invited – and indeed that resulted in – a refusal. The purchaser was held to forfeit the deposit that had been given.
24. Ref. *Healy* v. *Healy* [1973] Unrep. [H.C., R.I.].

11

The Standard Contract of Sale

INTRODUCTION

Most contracts of sale are entered into only with the professional advice of a solicitor. It is almost invariable therefore that such contracts be made in the standard form issued by the Incorporated Law Society of Ireland. The following is a consideration of the standard contract as revised in 1991.

PRELIMINARY

The preliminary part of the standard contract is prepared in such a way that brief particulars of the sale agreed may be noted thereon. The location of the property involved is included here. Also, there is reference to whether the sale is by private treaty or by auction. Provision is made for insertion of details of the auctioneer, where appropriate, and of the vendor's solicitor. Also, this part includes a recommendation that the contract should not be completed without prior legal advice.

CONSENT OF SPOUSE AND MEMORANDUM OF AGREEMENT

A form of consent to be completed by the spouse of the vendor for the purposes of section 3 of the Family Home

Protection Act, 1976, is contained on page one of the standard contract. If the property in sale is a family home within the meaning of that Act, the form of consent should be signed by the vendor's spouse prior to the agreement being signed by the vendor.

In compliance with the Statute of Frauds, a memorandum of agreement is also contained on page one. In this memorandum, it is agreed that the vendor shall sell, and that the purchaser shall purchase, the property described in the Particulars, in accordance with the annexed special and general conditions of sale. The date, parties, purchase price, deposit, closing date and the interest rate payable in the event of the purchaser defaulting on closing are specified in this memorandum. It is signed by both the vendor and the purchaser in the presence of witnesses, whose addresses and occupations are also specified. The memorandum also provides a form of receipt of the deposit, to be signed by the vendor's solicitor as stakeholder.

PARTICULARS AND TENURE

The particulars and tenure of the property in sale are inserted in the second page of the contract. A description of the property in sale, and the interest therein that the vendor is contracting to sell, is included here.

The description of the property should be such as to clearly identify the property contracted to be sold. Any imprecise descriptions, such as the "property pointed out and agreed between the parties hereto", should be avoided.

The description of the interest being sold may be quite brief, but should be precise. If the interest being sold is freehold, then the property should be described as, for instance, "held in fee simple". If it is leasehold, then the commencement date and term of the leasehold interest should be specified, together with the rent subject to which the property is held, and reference should be made to the lease wherein the covenants and conditions subject to which the property is held are contained.

If the property in sale is registered land, details should be given here, or in the special conditions, of any burdens that, under the Registration of Title Act, 1964, affect the land without registration; otherwise, the property may be regarded as not being subject to any such burdens.

SCHEDULES OF DOCUMENTS AND SEARCHES

Both of these schedules are provided for on page three of the standard contract. The documents schedule should specify all documents that have been available for inspection by the purchaser or his solicitor prior to the sale. These documents should include the root of title and all other documents of which the vendor wishes the purchaser to be on notice. In relation to registered land, it is normal to include an up to date copy folio and Land Registry map or file plan. When considering what documents should be included in this schedule, regard should be had to general condition number six.[1]

The searches schedule includes particulars of any searches that the vendor will procure and furnish to the purchaser. This schedule should be read together with general condition number nineteen.[2]

The searches schedule is drafted to envisage the possibility of a negative search in the Registry of Deeds on the index of names only for all acts affecting the subject property by the vendor. In practice, however, current searches are generally obtained by the purchaser.

1. See, infra, at page 143.
2. See, infra, at pages 146 and 147.

SPECIAL CONDITIONS

Provision for special conditions of sale is made on page four of the standard contract. Three standard special conditions are provided. The first incorporates in the special conditions the definitions and provisions as to interpretation contained in the general conditions.

The second special condition provides that the general conditions shall apply to the sale save in so far as they are altered or varied by the special conditions. It also provides that, in the event of any conflict, the special conditions shall prevail. Moreover, the second special condition negates the effect of any amendment to the general conditions unless the amendment is specifically referred to in the special conditions.

The third special condition provides for the payment to the vendor of the amount of any value added tax payable in relation to the sale.

In the remainder of page four of the standard contract, apart from the three standard special conditions, numerous other special conditions may be inserted. Such may include, for instance, restrictions imposed by the vendor on the investigation of title by the purchaser. Also, any conditions precedent to the completion of the sale should be inserted, for instance, conditions relating to loan sanction, planning permission or consents required under the Land Act, 1965. In addition, the special conditions should make provision for the title to be shown, since general condition 8 provides that the title to be shown shall be that set out in the special conditions.[3] Moreover, general conditions 11 and 12 deal with the issues of prior and intermediate title by reference to the special conditions.[4]

---

3. See, *infra*, at page 143.
4. See, *infra*, at page 144.

GENERAL CONDITIONS OF SALE

The remainder of the standard contract comprises fifty one general conditions of sale. The first three deal with matters of interpretation.

Condition 4 applies only if the sale is by auction. It provides for the division of the property into lots, a reserve price, a resolution of disputes as to bidding, bidding by the vendor, the withdrawal of the property and the payment of a deposit of ten per centum of the purchase price.

Condition 5 applies to sales by private treaty. It requires that the purchaser pay to the vendor's solicitor as stake-holder a deposit of the amount stated in the memorandum.

Condition 6 fixes the purchaser with notice of any covenants, conditions, rights, liabilities or restrictions contained in any lease or other document specified in the documents schedule. The import of this condition should be borne in mind in every sale, and all documents mentioned in the documents schedule carefully perused before contracts are signed or exchanged. The purchaser is fixed with notice of the contents of these documents, whether or not his solicitor has in fact inspected them.

Condition 7 requires the vendor, within seven working days of the date of sale, to deliver to the purchaser copies of the documents necessary to vouch the title to be shown. In practice, the vendor will usually have listed in the documents schedule all documents necessary to vouch title, in which event no further documents need be delivered pursuant to condition 7.

Condition 8 provides that the title to be shown by the vendor shall be such as is set forth in the special conditions.

Conditions 9 and 10 refer to the sale of leasehold property. Condition 9 precludes the investigation of the title of a grantor or lessor where the property in sale is leasehold.

This reflects the provisions contained in section 2 of the Vendor and Purchaser Act, 1874, and in section 3 of the Conveyancing Act, 1881.[5] Condition 10 refers to the objections or requisitions that may be raised by the purchaser concerning the leasehold interest in sale. It deals with discrepancies between a sub-lease and any superior lease on the title, and also provides for the receipt of the last gale of rent being accepted as conclusive evidence of the payment of all rent, and of compliance with all covenants and conditions in the lease.

Condition 10 also deals with the common problem of the lessor's consent to alienation. It provides that it is the vendor's obligation to procure the consent, and the purchaser must satisfy any reasonable requirements of the lessor in relation thereto. The vendor is not obliged to bring proceedings to secure the consent. However, where the consent has been refused, or has not been procured by the closing date and written evidence to this effect is furnished to the purchaser, or where the consent is issued subject to a condition that the purchaser on reasonable grounds refuses to accept, either party may rescind the sale by giving seven days notice in writing.

Conditions 11 and 12 limit the purchaser's investigation of title to deduction from the instrument specified as the commencement of title. They also preclude the investigation of title between instruments or events between which title is to pass.

Condition 13 is concerned exclusively with registered land. It provides for the discharge of equities, conversion of possessory title to absolute title, and for the delivery of an up to date copy folio and a Land Registry map or file plan. It refers to burdens that affect the land without registration, and the production of a land certificate in certain

---

5. See, infra, Chapter 12 at pages 158 and 159.

circumstances. It notes the obligation of the purchaser to procure himself to be registered as owner. Also, it provides that the vendor is not obliged to seek the removal of sporting rights reserved to the Land Commission.

In addition, Condition 13 requires the vendor to furnish a Land Registry folio and Land Registry map or file plan with the documents duly delivered in accordance with Condition 7. The production of such a map is essential if the purchaser is to satisfy himself that the title furnished relates to the property in sale.

The issue of the identity of the property in sale is dealt with in Condition 14. Effectively, this condition requires the purchaser to satisfy himself as to identity.

Conditions 15 and 16 deal with rights and liabilities that affect the property in sale and its actual state and condition. Condition 15 requires the vendor to disclose all easements, rights, privileges and liabilities known by him to affect the property in sale or that are likely to affect it. Condition 16 provides that, subject to Condition 15, the purchaser shall be deemed to buy with full notice of the actual state and condition of the property, and subject to all leases mentioned in the Particulars or the Special Conditions, and all rights of way, water, light, drainage and other easements, rights, reservations, privileges, liabilities, covenants, rents, outgoings and all incidents of tenure. In the event of any easements, rights, privileges, and liabilities referred to in condition 15 appearing in any documents of title, then, the inclusion of these documents in the Documents Schedule operates by virtue of the provisions of Condition 6[6] to satisfy the requirements of Condition 15.

Conditions 17 and 18 deal with requisitions of title. Condition 17 requires the purchaser to deliver his objections and requisitions on title within fourteen working days

---

6. See, supra, at page 143.

after the delivery to him of the copy documents of title set out in Condition 7.[7] Any objection or requisition not made within that time, and not going to the root of the title, is deemed to have been waived. The vendor is obliged to reply to the objections and requisitions within seven working days and, if he fails to do so, he is deemed to have accepted them as satisfactory. Condition 17 also requires the purchaser to raise any rejoinders arising on foot of the replies received within seven working days after the delivery thereof. Time is of the essence in this condition.

Condition 18 allows the vendor to rescind the contract in the event of the purchaser making and insisting on any objection or requisition as to the title, as to the assurance or as to other matters relating to and incidental to the sale, that the vendor is on the grounds of unreasonable delay or expense or other reasonable grounds, unable or unwilling to remove or comply with. The condition requires five working days notice of rescission, during which the purchaser has the option to withdraw the objection or requisition.

Condition 19 deals with searches, and should be read in conjunction with the Searches Schedule.[8] The condition requires the vendor to explain and discharge any acts appearing on searches covering the period in respect of which the title is to be deduced in accordance with the special conditions, but not outside of it, save in a case where an act appearing goes to the root of the title. In the case of acts appearing within the period for which title is to be deduced, the onus is on the vendor to show that they do not adversely affect the property in sale. In the event of a purchaser undertaking searches outside the period in respect of which title is to be shown, then, effectively, the

---

7. See, supra, at page 143.
8. See, supra, at page 141.

onus is on the purchaser to show that the act appearing affects the property in such a way as to go to the root of the title before he can call on the vendor to explain or discharge same.

Condition 20 deals with the assurance of the property. It requires the draft deed to be submitted to the vendor's solicitor not less than seven working days before the closing date, and the engrossment to be so delivered not less than four working days before the closing date. The delivery of a draft deed or engrossment does not prejudice any outstanding objection or requisition validly made.

Condition 21 entitles the purchaser to vacant possession of the property in sale on completion of the sale, subject to any provisions to the contrary in the Particulars, or in the Special Conditions, or implied by the nature of the transaction.

Conditions 22 and 23 apply where the property in sale is sold subject to a lease. Details of any such lease or tenancy should be made available to the purchaser or his solicitor prior to the sale. If the terms of a lease or tenancy are contained in a lease or letting agreement, it is advisable that this document be included in the Documents Schedule so as to avoid any dispute as to whether or not the requirements of this condition have been complied with.

Condition 23 entitles the purchaser to assume that, at the date of the sale, the lessee named in the sale is the actual lessee, that no variation has occurred in the terms of the lease and that such terms have been complied with. The detailed provisions of condition 23 clearly indicate that the principle of "caveat emptor" is not displaced, and that the condition does not relieve a purchaser from having to inspect the condition of the property.

Conditions 24 to 26 deal with the completion of the contract, and the payment of interest in the event of the purchaser defaulting in closing on the appointed day. Condition 24 states that the sale shall be completed, and the balance of the purchase price paid by the purchaser, on or before the closing date. It also provides that completion shall take place at the office of the vendor's solicitor.

Condition 25 makes provision for the payment of interest by the purchaser on the balance of the purchase monies if the closing of the sale is delayed by any default on his part. Interest is payable from either:– the contractual closing date or such subsequent date thereafter when delay in completing is not attributable to any default on behalf of the vendor, whichever date is the later. An alternative open to the vendor is to elect to take the rents and profits less the outgoings of the property up to the date of completion.

Condition 26 allows the vendor to make proper preparation for completion, including the furnishing of an apportionment account, without prejudicing his rights under condition 25 in the event of the purchaser defaulting.

Condition 27 must be read in conjunction with the definition of "apportionment date" contained in condition 2.[9] The condition deals with the purchaser's entitlement to possession of the property in sale, and the apportionment of rents and profits and outgoings. All relevant sums must be apportioned on a day to day basis, whether apportionable by law or not. This means that if there are any monies payable periodically to or by the owner of property in respect of it, these monies shall be apportioned on a time basis between the vendor and the purchaser. If precise figures are not available on the closing date, fair estimates

---

9. The Apportionment Date means "either (a) the later of (i) the closing date. . . and (ii) such subsequent date from which delay in completing the sale shall cease to be attributable to default on the part of the Vendor or (b) in the event of the Vendor exercising the right to elect referred to in Condition 25 hereunder, the date of actual completion of the sale or (c) such other date as may be agreed by the Vendor and the Purchaser to be the Apportionment Date for the purpose of this definition."

shall be made for the purpose of ascertaining the amount payable on closing and, later, when the actual figures are ascertained, a difference arising between them and the previous estimates met by either the vendor or the purchaser as appropriate.

Condition 28 deals with the situation where section 45 of the Land Act, 1965, applies to a sale. It is for the purchaser to procure any certificate or consent necessary. If the section applies, it is imperative that the purchaser inserts a special condition making the sale subject to the issue of the required certificate or consent.

If the land is unregistered land, the registration of which is compulsory on completion, Condition 29 provides that it is a matter for the purchaser to procure same. The condition also requires the vendor to supply any additional information required that he is reasonably able to supply, if requested, and the purchaser must pay the vendor's expenses of complying with any such request. It is notable that the terms of this condition do not operate to impose on the vendor any obligation to provide a better title than that required to be shown under the contract.

Condition 30 deals with the situation where a purchaser signs "in trust" or "as agent", and reiterates the principle of the personal liability of an agent acting for an undisclosed principal.

Conditions 31 and 32 deal with a failure by the purchaser to pay the deposit. If the purchaser does not pay the deposit, the vendor may terminate the sale or sue the purchaser for damages, or both, without prejudice to any rights otherwise available to him. If the deposit is paid by a cheque that is dishonoured, Condition 32 entitles the vendor to treat the contract as having been discharged by breach, or to sue on the cheque, or otherwise to enforce payment of the deposit.

Condition 33 deals with a situation where there has

been some error, omission or mis-statement regarding the property in sale, whether in quantity, quality, tenure or otherwise.[10] The condition provides that the purchaser will not be obliged to accept, or the vendor to assure, property differing substantially from that agreed to be sold, unless the purchaser or vendor, as the case may be, would not be prejudiced materially by reason of the difference. However, no error, save a substantial error that materially prejudices the other party, entitles the vendor or purchaser to set the sale aside. That does not however mean that compensation may not be payable. If a purchaser suffers loss as a result of an error communicated by the vendor, he is entitled to compensation from the vendor. He is not however entitled to compensation in respect of any matter of which he is deemed to have notice under condition 16 (a) in relation to an error in a map or plan furnished for identification purposes.[11]

Condition 34 determines the respective rights of the vendor and purchaser with respect to the original title documents, when the vendor is selling part only of the property he holds under any given title. This condition is of practical significance only in respect of unregistered land. In relation to such land, the vendor retains the original title documents but must provide the purchaser with certified copies of the documents retained, save documents of record of which he need only give plain copies. In addition, the vendor must give a statutory acknowlededment of the right of production, and an undertaking for the safe custody, of the documents retained. Documents of record need not be made the subject of acknowledgement or undertaking.

---

10. The term "error" as used in the contract is widely defined as including any mistake, omission, discrepancy, misrepresentation, and so forth, whether made during the pre-contract negotiations or contained in the contract itself.

11. See, supra, at page 145.

Where part only of unregistered land is being sold, this condition also requires a stamped and registered counterpart of the deed of assurance to be prepared by the purchaser at his expense and delivered to the vendor.

Condition 35, which deals with the question of the disclosure of notices, is of critical importance. It entitles the purchaser to rescind the sale if he did not receive or was not made aware of certain specified notices prior to the date of sale.[12] In general, the type of notices referred to in the condition concern those given under legislation on housing, planning and compulsory purchase.

Under Condition 36, the vendor warrants that the property has any planning permission and bye-law approval necessary to its existing use. It requires the vendor to furnish, together with the title documents, copies of relevant planning permissions and building bye-law approvals, and on completion to furnish evidence of compliance with same.

Conditions 37, 38 and 39 apply where the sale is rescinded. Condition 37 provides for the restoration of both parties to their original positions by the return of the deposit and documentation, and the removal of any entries in any official registers. If the deposit is not returned within five working days, Condition 38 requires the vendor to pay interest at the stipulated interest rate to the purchaser; otherwise, no interest is payable. Condition 39 permits negotiations and attempts at settlement of a dispute without prejudicing any right to rescind.

Condition 40 is one of the most important of the general conditions. It deals with the issue of completion notices in

---

12. The term "date of sale" is defined in General Condition 2 as "the date of the auction when the sale shall have been by auction, and otherwise means the date upon which the contract for the sale shall have become binding on the Vendor and the Purchaser."

the event of a sale not being completed on or before the closing date. This condition applies only where time is not of the essence in respect of the closing date and accordingly, if the contract contains a special condition making time of the essence, or if time is deemed to be of the essence on any other grounds, this condition does not apply. In order that this condition be applicable, one party must be able, ready and willing to complete the sale, or is not so by reason of the default or misconduct of the other party. The party seeking completion must serve on the other party a notice to complete the sale in accordance with the condition. On service of such notice, the sale must be closed within twenty eight days, in respect of which period time is of the essence. If the purchaser does not comply with the notice, the provisions of condition 41 allowing the forfeiture of his deposit may be enforced, or the vendor may exercise any other rights and remedies, such as suing for specific performance or damages for breach of contract. If it is the vendor who is in default, the purchaser may exercise his rights at law or in equity, or require the return of his deposit. If he requires the return of his deposit, and obtains it, he is no longer entitled to claim specific performance, but may claim damages for breach of contract. Condition 40(g) was first introduced in 1988. It is designed to rebut any allegation that the vendor is not able, ready and willing to complete the sale in specific situations commonly encountered in practice.

Condition 41 allows the vendor to forfeit the purchaser's deposit in specific circumstances. Forfeiture is permissible if the purchaser fails in a material respect to comply with the conditions of sale. This condition is most often invoked following the service of a notice under condition 40. Its application is not however confined to those circumstances, but also applies if the purchaser fails in any other material respect to comply with the conditions. If the deposit is forfeited, the vendor may resell the property. If he does so within one year after the contractual closing date, he may claim against the purchaser for any loss, costs or expenses arising, but must allow credit for the deposit. Condition 42 preserves the parties' rights to damages where an order for specific performance is obtained but not complied with.

Condition 43 was first introduced in the 1988 standard contract for sale, and it reverses the common law position as to the passing of risk. It provides that the vendor shall be liable for any loss or damage occasioned between the date of sale and the actual completion of the sale, although the amount of any such liability shall not exceed the purchase price. Condition 44 operates to limit the liability thus imposed on the vendor to exclude liability for inconsequential damage, or damage arising from the vacating of the property by the vendor, or damage arising from compliance with obligations imposed by certain state bodies.

Condition 45 preserves certain rights and liabilities of the parties, notwithstanding the reversal of the common law rule as to the passing of risk in condition 43.

Condition 46 imposes on the vendor a warranty that any chattels included in the sale are unencumbered, and not subject to any lease, purchase or other such agreement. Condition 47 permits the purchaser to inspect the subject property, including chattels, at reasonable times and on a reasonable number of occasions.

Condition 48 preserves all obligations designed to survive or capable of surviving completion from the effect of the doctrine of merger, under which after closing the rights of the parties in certain circumstances are limited to the rights and liabilities arising on the assurance of the property.[13]

Condition 49 deals with the issue of notices, and

13.　See, supra, Chapter 10 at page 135.

condition 50 deals with time limits.

Condition 51 is the final general condition in the standard contract. It provides for arbitration in relation to certain listed differences and disputes arising between vendor and purchaser.

12

Title to be Shown Under an Open Contract

INTRODUCTION

Parties to contracts of sale normally contract for a specific title. In the event however of a contract that is open on the question of title, both the root and period of title that the purchaser may require are matters governed by statute and by common law. It is proposed here to consider the relevant principles, including those peculiar to leasehold unregistered title.

SEARCHING TITLE TO UNREGISTERED FREEHOLD PROPERTY

1. The Period of Title

Before 1874, a vendor was generally stated to be under a duty to show a "good title". The rule of thumb adopted was that the vendor should produce evidence as to the title going back sixty years.

The Vendor and Purchaser Act, 1874, legislated for the period of title that now has to be shown under an open contract:–

"In the completion of any contract of sale of land made after 1874, and subject to any stipulation to the contrary in the contract, forty years shall be substituted as the period of commencement of title which a purchaser may require in the place of sixty years."[1]

2. Roots of Title

Irrespective of the period of title that a vendor must show, it is essential that the commencement of the period of title shown should lie in a good root of title:–

"The root of title must be an instrument of disposition, either dealing with or proving on the face of it, without the aid of extrinsic evidence, the ownership of the entire legal and equitable interest in the property sold, containing a description by which the property can be identified, and showing nothing to cast any doubt on the title of the disposing party."[2]

The relative marketability of a root of title depends on the extent to which it proves that the vendor or his predecessors in title had ownership of the property. The following is a classification of roots of title into "good" and "doubtful" respectively:–

Good Roots of Title

1. The best root is one that lies in an Act of Parliament.[3]
2. A conveyance for value.
3. A legal mortgage in fee simple.
4. A pre-marital settlement of property made in consideration either of money or marriage. A post-marital settlement of property is not beyond doubt.

---

1. Vendor and Purchaser Act, 1874, s. 1.
2. Williams, *Vendor and Purchaser*, (4th. ed.) at page 124.
3. Titles registered under the Registration of Title Act, 1964, are in this category.

5. A deed of either exchange or partition made since 1845 and not made under the Inclosure Acts.
6. A testamentary devise of specific property to a specific devisee where it is proved that the testator had seisin at his death.
7. A deed of appointment that recites the power under which the appointment is made.
8. A disentailing assurance, but only when the actual entail is cited and produced.

Doubtful Roots of Title

1. Voluntary Deeds.
2. Post-marital settlements.
3. A legal mortgage by demise or sub-demise.
4. A general testamentary devise.
5. New fee farm grants.

SEARCHING TITLE TO UNREGISTERED LEASEHOLD PROPERTY

1. Period of Title

Section 1 of the Vendor and Purchaser Act, 1874, also applies to leaseholds, so that the vendor of a leasehold interest under an open contract must prove title for forty years. However, if the leasehold interest that is being purchased dates from a lease that is more than forty years old, the vendor should produce, and the purchaser should insist upon, the lease itself in order to show what its terms are.

Where the lease is more than forty years old, the purchaser should insist on obtaining the lease, and the next oldest document that the purchaser should insist upon would be a root of title that is at least forty years old. The acceptance of a root of title that is less than forty years old is dangerous; any interests that arose on the title during the previous forty years, and that the purchaser would have discovered if he had insisted upon deduction of title for the full period, can bind the purchaser.[4]

2. Summary of Task in Investigation of Title to Unregistered Leasehold Property

The task of a person purchasing an unregistered leasehold interest may be summarised as follows:– first, he should seek the lease out of which his interest is to be carved; secondly, he should start with a root of title that is at least forty years old;[5] and thirdly, he should trace the title up to the present.

3. Statutory Provisions that may Restrict the Investigation

It is now necessary to consider three statutory provisions that can restrict a person who is purchasing a leasehold interest from complying with the foregoing task of examination of title.

(1) The first restrictive provision is contained in section 2 of the Vendor and Purchaser Act, 1874:–

> "Under a contract to grant or assign a term of years, whether derived or to be derived out of a freehold or leasehold estate, the intended lessee or assignee shall not be entitled to call for the title to the freehold."

This section may prevent the following purchasers of a leasehold interest from demanding the freehold root:– first,

---

4. This is commonly referred to as the rule in *Patman* v. *Harland* [1881] 17 Ch. D. 353.
5. Vendor and Purchaser Act, 1874, s. 1.

the taker of a first lease; secondly, an assignee of the first lease; thirdly, a sub-lessee under a first lease; and fourthly, an assignee of a sublease.

(2) A second restrictive provision is contained in section 3(1) of the Conveyancing Act, 1881:

> "Under a contract to sell or assign a term of years derived out of a leasehold interest in land, the intended assignee shall not have the right to call for the title to the leasehold reversion."

This provision prevents an assignee of a sub-lease from demanding the title documents to the leasehold reversion.

(3) A third restrictive provision is contained in section 13(1) of the Conveyancing Act, 1881:–

> "On a contract to grant a lease for a term of years to be derived out of a leasehold interest with a leasehold reversion, the intended lessee shall not have the right to call for the title to the leasehold reversion."

This provision prevents a sub-lessee from demanding the title documents to the leasehold reversion.

The above sections apply only in relation to open contracts. They limit the title documents that a purchaser of an unregistered leasehold interest can demand of the vendor. A purchaser caught by these provisions runs a risk under the rule in *Patman* v. *Harland.*[6]

In practice, the sections may be avoided in two ways. First, the provisions of a formal contract can exclude the sections. Secondly, practitioners can co-operate among themselves despite the sections.

---

6. See, supra, at page 158.

BAD ROOTS OF TITLE
VENDOR'S DUTY OF DISCLOSURE

A purchaser of either freehold or leasehold, irrespective of the period of title to be produced, is entitled to assume that the vendor will produce a good root of title. Furthermore, any provisions restricting a purchaser from seeking a good root of title must be fair and explicit. Otherwise, a purchaser who is offered a bad root of title can refuse to complete the sale.

A vendor in one case offered a voluntary conveyance as a root of title.[7] The contract had provided that the title should commence with a deed thirty years old, but had not referred to the nature of the deed. It was held that the purchaser was justified in refusing to complete unless title was shown for the full forty years. The basis of the decision was that any conditions restricting a purchaser's right to investigate title as required by law should be fair and explicit. Also, the court stated that if a contract contains a condition providing for the commencement of title with a deed less than forty years old, then the purchaser is entitled to assume that the agreed root of title is a conveyance for value.

---

7. *Re Marsh and Earl Glanville*, 24 Ch.D. 11.

13

Consents Required under the Land Act, 1965

INTRODUCTION

The potential application of sections 12 and 45 of the Land Act, 1965, requires to be considered in every sale of land. When appropriate, the consents and certificates required by these provisions will be dealt with in special conditions of the contract of sale. Also, the provisions will be the subject of requisitions and replies thereto. Finally, compliance with the provisions, when relevant, will be noted by statutory declaration in the conveyance or other instrument of disposition.

SECTION 12, LAND ACT, 1965

This section provides that an agricultural holding shall not be let, sub-let or sub-divided without the written consent of the Minister.[1] Such consent may be either general or particular, and may be subject to conditions.

The term agricultural, as used in the section, means substantially either agricultural or pastoral.

---

1. The Land Commission was abolished by section 2 of the Irish Land Commission (Dissolution) Act, 1992. Its functions were dispersed under sections 3 and 4 of the Act between the High Court and the Minister for Agriculture and Food.

The section is a device of agricultural land planning. It enables the Minister by withholding consent to letting, sub-letting or sub-division to promote optimum size agricultural holdings. The Minister may withhold a section 12 consent only to prevent the creation or continuance of holdings that are not economic. Any purported disposition in breach of the section is void. Provision exists, however, for a retrospective validation.

Exclusion from Section 12 of Certain Agricultural Land

The section does not apply to any holding:-

1. That is not subject to a purchase annuity or other sum payable to the Minister; and
2. Either
   (a) The entire holding is within the boundary of any county borough, borough, urbn district or town; or
   (b) The Minister certifies that such holding is - by virtue of its proximity to a county borough, borough, urban district or town -required for urban development.

Vendor's Responsibility

The vendor is responsible for obtaining any necessary section 12 consent. A special condition should therefore be included in the contract of sale to protect him against the refusal of consent.

General Consent Procedure

The Land Commission introduced a general consent procedure in 1977, that was amended on July 1, 1980. This applies, with certain exceptions, to registered agricultural holdings where the severed plots do not exceed one hectare in size. A particular consent is not necessary in dealings within the general consent procedure.

Dealings covered by the general consent are subject to two conditions:-

1. The purchaser must be a qualified person under section 45 of the Land Act, 1965, and he must be so certified in the transfer deed; and

2. The severed plot must be discharged from any land purchase annuity or land reclamation annuity. The balance of the holding will remain charged with the entire annuity.

By way of exceptions, the general consent procedure does not apply to dealings to which any of the following circumstances, set out in paragraph 6, is referable:-

1. If the Minister has notified the owner or his solicitor of proceedings under the Land Act for acquisition of the holding, in whole or in part.

2. If, on the severance of a plot, the balance of the holding, excluding any undivided commonage would be less than two hectares in extent; this circumstance does not exclude from the general consent any holdings not subject to land purchase, or land reclamation, annuity.

3. Where subdivisions aggregating in excess of two hectares are attempted or effected under the general consent procedure; here again, this circumstance will not exclude from the general consent any holdings not subject to land purchase, or land reclamation, annuity. It may be noted that multiple subdivisions under the general consent are conditional on the severed plots being transferred to different parties.

4. If the severed plot contains any existing buildings other than:- (a) old buildings which are uninhabited and unused; or (b) any building newly erected or in course of erection pursuant to the current subdivision transaction.

5. If the holding to be subdivided comprises a Land Commission Trust Scheme - pasturage or tillage, sportsfield, playground, or the like - set up pursuant to the Irish Land Act, 1903, and the Land Act, 1950.

6. If the holding to be subdivided has been involved in exchange proceedings with the Land Commission and where the exchanged lands are awaiting revesting.

In subdivisions coming within the general consent procedure, the transfer document must contain a certificate in the following form:

"It is hereby certified that Folio No. ....
County .... herein is not affected by any of the circumstances listed in paragraph 6 of the general consent dated 1 July, 1980 (SR/77)."

The general consent procedure greatly altered conveyancing practice in relation to section 12 of the Land Act, 1965. For instance, it obviates the need in many cases for a particular consent on the sale of individual building sites.

SECTION 45, LAND ACT, 1965

Section 45 provides that no interest in land shall vest in a person who is not a qualified person unless he obtains the written consent of the Minister. The section implements the general policy that Irish farm land should not ordinarily pass into the control of non-nationals.

Non-application of Section 45 to Certain Land

The section does not apply to land situate in a county borough, borough, urban district or town.[2]

---

2. Land Act, 1965, s. 45(1).

Exclusion from Consent Requirements of Certain Vestings

The consent requirements, by virtue of section 45(2)(B), do not apply to the vesting of interests in the following:-

1. A State Authority.
    A State Authority means:
    (a) a Minister of State,
    (b) the Revenue Commissioners, and
    (c) the Commissioners of Public Works in Ireland;
2. A person as legal personal representative of a deceased person; and
3. A member of the family on the distribution of the estate of a deceased person.

Qualified Persons

The concept of the qualified person is central in the application of section 45. The categories of persons who are qualified are contained in section 45(1) and in five statutory instruments introduced under that provision.

The categories of persons set out in section 45(1) as being qualified are as follows:-

1. Irish citizens,
2. A person, other than a body corporate, who has been ordinarily resident in the State continuously during the seven years ending at the material time,
3. A person certified by the Minister of Industry, Commerce and Energy as having shown to the Minister's satisfaction that he is acquiring an interest exclusively for the purpose of an industry other than agriculture,
4. A local authority,
5. A body corporate which, under the Companies Act, 1963, is registered without the addition of the word "limited",

6.   A body corporate established by statute,

7.   A body corporate established under a specific statutory direction or authorisation,

8.   A bank named in the Third Schedule to the Central Bank Act, 1942,

9.   A person certified by the Minister as having shown to his satisfaction that he is acquiring an interest for private residential purposes where the land involved does not exceed five acres in extent, and

10.   Any additional category declared by regulation by the Minister for Lands.

An additional category of qualified persons was declared by the Minister for Lands by statutory instrument number 4 of 1970. That regulation provided that a person acquiring an interest in land that is situate in a town specified in part two of the first schedule of the Local Government (Planning and Development) Act, 1963, shall be a qualified person.[3]

Moreover, additional categories of qualified persons were declared by the Minister for Lands by statutory instrument number 322 of 1972. That regulation constitutes as qualified persons certain beneficiaries under various directives of the E.C. The main provisions of these directives are as follows:-

1.   farms, that have been abandoned or left uncultivated in any member state, may be acquired by nationals of other member states;

2.   nationals of one member state, who have worked continuously for at least two years as paid agricultural workers in another member state, may acquire farms in that state;

---

3.   The relevant part of the schedule lists fifty eight towns.

3. a national of any member state, who has been engaged in farming for more than two years, may exchange his farm for one in another member state;

4. a national of any member state may avail of the rural lease system, if any, in another member state; and

5. a national of any member state, who is self-employed in forestry or logging, may purchase wooded land or forestry soils for forestry purposes in another member state.

An additional category of qualified persons was declared by the Minister for Agriculture by statutory instrument number 144 of 1983. Under that instrument, a "qualified person" shall include a person who is a citizen of a member state of the European Communities and who:-

"(a) is exercising in the State the right of establishment as a self-employed person under Article 52 of the E.C. Treaty,[4] by way of an economic activity the nature of which is specified in the relevant certificate given by that person under subsection (3) of the said section 45, and

(b) is acquiring an interest in land to which the said section 45 applies for the purpose of or in connection with such exercise of that right."

Further categories of qualified persons, that have already been referred to in the Preface, were created by S.I. No. 67 of 1994 and S.I. No. 56 of 1995.

Any person acquiring land that is covered by section 45, by a vesting to which the section applies, need not obtain a ministerial consent if he is a qualified person within the foregoing categories. It may be noted

---

4. The Treaty was adopted in Ireland by the European Communities Act, 1972 (No. 27 of 1972).

however that two of these categories[5] are dependent on prior certifications, by the Minister for Industry, Commerce and Energy, and by the Minister for Agriculture and Food, respectively.

Purchaser's Responsibility

The purchaser bears responsibility for obtaining, where relevant, a section 45 consent. To protect him against the possibility of the consent not forthcoming, a special condition should be inserted in the standard contract.

Miscellaneous Provisions in the Section

An instrument of disposition, containing one of the four certificates referred to in section 45(3)(a), shall effect a vesting notwithstanding any objection to the accuracy of such vesting. Also, a ministerial consent may be given retrospectively.[6]

The Minister, if he is of opinion that a non qualified person has acquired possession, occupation or control of land within the section, without having obtained the necessary consent, may serve a notice for particulars on such person .[7] Moreover, where control of a body corporate, in which land within the section is vested, is transferred to a non-qualified person, the body corporate is under a duty to notify the Minister within one month from such transfer. The Minister may then acquire the land.[8]

Criminal sanctions are provided for false or misleading statements made in connection with the section.[9]

---

5. Numbers 3 and 9 of those listed in s. 45(1), *supra* at pages 165 and 166.
6. Land Act, 1965, s. 45(9)(a).
7. Land Act, 1965, s. 45(4).
8. Land Act, 1965, s. 45(5).
9. Land Act, 1965, s. 45(6), (7) and (8).

14

Form and Effect of a Conveyance of a Fee Simple

THE DEED AS A CONVEYANCING INSTRUMENT

The principal methods for conveying hereditaments prior to 1845 were as follows:– feoffment with livery of seisin; lease and release at common law; lease and release under the Statute of Uses; and fines and recoveries.

Each of the foregoing methods of conveyancing suffered from various disadvantages. Consequently, the Real Property Act, 1845, made it possible to convey an hereditament in possession by deed.

MEANING OF CONVEYANCE

A conveyance, in its general sense, may be defined as "an instrument that operates to pass an interest in property from one person to another". The form of a conveyance is variable. It depends on whether freehold or leasehold property is involved and, in the case of leasehold, it depends on whether the alienation is by sub-demise or assignment.

FORM OF A CONVEYANCE OF A FEE SIMPLE

The outline and order of the parts of a conveyance of a fee simple have become almost invariable, and have acquired some legal significance. Also, since its composition is illustrative of the form and import of other dispositive deeds, it is now considered in brief outline.

1. Commencement and Date

The traditional practice is to commence a conveyance with the words "This Indenture". In modern practice, however, a conveyance is sometimes commenced with words that describe the general nature of the document, for instance, "This Conveyance", "This Mortgage", and so forth.

A deed takes effect from the date upon which it is signed, sealed and delivered by the grantor. There is a presumption that the date in a deed is the date of delivery. This presumption may however be rebutted by proof that the deed was delivered at some date other than the date cited.[1] The date in a conveyance is also important in connection with stamping. The general rule contained in the Stamp Act, 1891, is that instruments should be stamped before execution. Section 15(2) of that Act however enables certain specified instruments, including a conveyance, to be stamped or presented for adjudication without payment of a penalty within thirty days after they have been executed.

2. Parties

Every essential party to a transaction must be included as a party. Thus, for instance, if property that is mortgaged is being sold free from the mortgage, the mortgagee should be joined as a party.

3. Recitals

Recitals are of two types, namely, narrative and intro-

---

1. See, e.g., Browne v. Burton [1847] 17 L.J., Q.B. 49 at page 50.

ductory. Narrative recitals deal with matters relating to how the grantor became entitled to the property. Narrative recitals may be either general or particular, depending on the degree of specificity with which they describe how the grantor became entitled to the property.

Introductory recitals are "a preliminary statement of what the maker of the deed intended should be the effect and purpose of the whole deed when made".[2] The introductory recitals are based, generally, on the terms of the contract of sale.

4. *Testatum*

This is the beginning of the operative part of a conveyance, and usually consists of such words as "Now This Indenture Witnesseth".

5. *Consideration*

Consideration is not essential to a deed. Consideration, however, should be stated if it exists in order to show that the transaction is not a voluntary one.

6. *Receipt Clause*

The receipt clause normally consists of such words as "the receipt whereof is hereby acknowledged". The principal reason for such a clause is that it dispenses with the need to give a separate receipt for the purchase money.

Also, a solicitor who produces a conveyance containing such a clause that has been executed by the vendor thereby shows the purchaser that he has authority from the vendor to receive the purchase money.

---

2. Per Lord Hallsbury in *Re MacKensie* v. *Duke of Devonshire* [1896] A.C. 400 at page 406.

7. Operative Words

The operative words effect the actual conveyance of the property. Following is an illustration:– "The Vendor, as beneficial owner, hereby conveys to the purchaser". The statement of the capacity in which the vendor sells – for instance, as beneficial owner, as settlor, or as trustee – is important since it determines the covenants for title that will be implied in a conveyance under the Conveyancing Act, 1881.

8. Parcels

The parcels describe the property that is being transferred. This part of a conveyance usually commences with such words as "All That And Those".

9. Habendum

"To hold the same unto the purchaser in fee simple" are the words that traditionally follow the parcels clause in a conveyance of a fee simple. Coke stated that, "The habendum has two parts: first, to name again the feofee, and, secondly, to limit the certainty of the estate".

Whereas it is the function of the parcels clause to determine the physical quantum of land passing, it is the function of the habendum to determine the quantum of the estate in that land that the grantee or purchaser will take.

It is unnecessary to use the words "unto and to the use of the purchaser" in the habendum, unless the deed is voluntary; in such latter case, these words rebut the presumption of a resulting use in favour of the grantor.

10. Covenants and Reservations

Covenants and reservations are unusual in conveyances of freeholds. They are common, however, in the case of conveyances of fee farm grants and of leases.

An almost infinite variety of covenants is possible, and the general rule is that they will "run with the land". It is common in this part of the conveyance also to have an indemnity clause, whereby the vendor agrees to indemnify the purchaser against the breach of any covenants or reservations provided for.

11. Acknowledgment and Undertaking

This part is necessary where a purchaser is buying only a portion of property. It normally consists of a clause such as the following:–

> "The vendor hereby acknowledges the right of the purchaser to the production of the documents specified in the schedule hereto (the possession of which is retained by the vendor) and to delivery of copies thereof and hereby undertakes with the purchaser for the safe custody thereof."

12. Statutory Certificates

This part of a conveyance will contain certificates in accordance with statutes such as the Stamp Act, 1891, the Land Act, 1965, and the Family Home Protection Act, 1976. The "certificate of value" is the relevant certificate under the Stamp Act, 1891. That Act provides that stamp duty on a conveyance or transfer on sale will be charged at a reduced rate where the consideration does not exceed a specified amount and the instrument is certified at that amount. The certificate must consist of "a statement certifying that the transaction effected by the instrument does not form part of a larger transaction, or series of transactions, in respect of which the amount or value, or aggregate amount or value, of the consideration exceeds that amount."

A certificate may be inserted with reference to section 12 of the Land Act, 1965. For instance:–

"It is hereby certified that a consent has been obtained under section 12 of the Land Act, 1965, and that the conditions attaching to this consent have been complied with."

It is usual to have a certificate with reference to section 45 of the Land Act, 1965. For instance,

"It is hereby certified that the grantee has obtained an appropriate consent under section 45(2) of the Land Act, 1965, and that any conditions attached to that consent have been complied with."

Finally, a certificate may be included with reference to the Family Home Protection Act, 1976. For instance:–

"It is hereby certified that the property the subject of the foregoing deed and purported to be hereby transferred is subject to the provisions of the Family Home Protection Act, 1976, and that the consent of the spouse of the grantor for the purpose of Section 3 of that Act has been given."

13. Testimonium and Attestation

Traditionally, the ultimate part of a deed is the testimonium. The following form, which is typical, is self-explanatory:–

"In Witness Whereof the parties hereto have hereunto set their hands and seals the day and year first before written."

COVENANTS FOR TITLE

It was common before 1881 to include in conveyances lengthy covenants regarding title. The need for express inclusion disappeared to some extent with the passing of the Conveyancing Act, 1881: section 7 of that Act provides that certain covenants will be implied in every conveyance by deed.

Although the implied covenants constitute a useful safeguard for the purchaser, he is usually protected against defects in his title by an extensive investigation of title prior to completion of the sale.

Operation of the Covenants

The covenants are implied provided that:–

A. the conveyance is by deed,
B. the conveyance is for valuable consideration, and
C. the vendor is expressed to convey as beneficial owner. The use of certain other phrases other than "as beneficial owner" also incorporate, as will be seen, certain covenants.

The implied covenants, as regards freeholds, concern the following:–

1. Full power to convey
   The vendor has a right to convey the interest agreed to be sold.[3]
2. Quiet enjoyment
   The purchaser shall have quiet enjoyment of the land.[4]
3. Freedom from encumbrances
   The land shall be enjoyed free from any encum-

---

3. Conveyancing Act, 1881, s. 7(1)(a).
4. See, e.g., *Howard* v. *Maitland* [1883] 11 Q.B.D. 695.

brances, other than those subject to which the conveyance is made.[5]

4. Further assurances

The vendor will execute such assurances, and carry out such acts, as are necessary to remedy any defect in the conveyance.[6]

The following covenants, in addition to the foregoing, are implied in the case of leaseholds:–

5. Lease current

The lease is valid and subsisting.

6. Covenants performed

The rent has been paid to date, and the other covenants in the lease have been duly performed.

The number of covenants implied in any given conveyance depends on the capacity in which the grantor is expressed to convey the property. All the covenants are implied where the grantor is expressed to convey as beneficial owner. Where the grantor conveys as settlor, only the covenant on further assurances is implied. None of the covenants set out previously is implied where the grantor conveys as mortgagee, as personal representative, as committee, as receiver or under an order of the court; in these instances, the only covenant implied is that the grantor has not himself encumbered the property.

Enforceability of the Covenants

The benefit of the implied covenants runs with the land. The burden of the covenants is personal, and binds only the covenantor, his heirs and estate.

The covenants, in general, extend only to acts and

---

5. See, e.g., *Turner* v. *Moon* [1901] 2 Ch. 825 at 828.
6. See, e.g., *Maguire* v. *Armstrong* [1814] 2 Ba. and B. 538.

omissions of the covenantor himself, anyone claiming through, under or in trust for him, and anyone through whom he claims otherwise than by purchase for money or money's worth.

Finally, assuming that full covenants are given on each sale, a purchaser will normally get the benefit of a chain of covenants given by all previous vendors of the land.

PRACTICE AFTER COMPLETION

It has already been remarked that a number of important items will require attention by or on behalf of the purchaser after the closing of a sale.[7] Thus, for instance, the rating authority should be notified of the change of ownership. Also, the purchaser will arrange permanent insurance on the property purchased.

Two further matters that may also require to be attended will now be considered in more detail. First, the conveyance from vendor to purchaser may need to be registered under the Registry of Deeds system.[8] Secondly, a mortgage of the property purchased may need to be executed where the purchase has been financed by a loan.

Registration of Conveyance under Registry of Deeds System

A purchaser of unregistered property will have searched in the Registry of Deeds in order to ascertain the encumbrances if any that have been registered against the vendor. If the searches disclosed any encumbrances – such as a mortgage – these will have been discharged by completion, unless the intention was that the property be taken subject to them.

---

7. See, supra, Chapter 9 at pages 126 and 127.
8. For elaboration on this aspect, see, infra, Chapter 17 at page 214 et seq.

After completion, it is almost invariable practice for the purchaser to register the newly acquired deed of conveyance. Such registration, although not compulsory, ensures priority for the purchaser. Such registration is effected by submitting to the Registry of Deeds the following documents:

1. the conveyance duly executed and stamped,
2. a memorial of the conveyance, and
3. an affidavit of due execution of the conveyance and the memorial sworn by a common witness of both documents.

The memorial must contain the date of the conveyance, the names, addresses and descriptions of the parties thereto, and of the witnesses, one of whom must have been a witness to the execution of the deed.[9] It must also contain a statement of the effect of the conveyance. Following is a precedent memorial of a fee simple conveyance:–

"To the Registrar for Registering Deeds and soforth in Ireland.

A MEMORIAL of Indenture of Conveyance dated the .... day of .... 19..... BETWEEN John Murphy of.......... (therein and hereinafter called "the Vendor") of the one part and John Twomey of.......... (therein and hereinafter called "the Purchaser") of the other part WHEREBY it was witnessed that in consideration of the sum of £42,000 (payable as therein) and of the covenants on the part of the Purchaser therein inserted the Vendor as beneficial owner did thereby convey unto the purchaser ALL THAT AND THOSE part of the property in the Townland of Rath, Barony

---

9. See also Registration of Deeds Act, 1707, s. 7, and the Registry of Deeds (Ireland) Act, 1832, s. 29.

of East Carbery, County of Cork, and consisting of four acres and a dwelling house thereon more particularly delineated on the map endorsed on the said Indenture of Conveyance and thereon surrounded by a red verge line TO HOLD the same unto and to the use of the purchaser in fee simple AND which said Indenture of Conveyance and this Memorial as to the due execution thereof by the said John Murphy was witnessed by Brian Swift of .... and Bob Jones of .... AND which said Indenture of Conveyance as to the due execution thereof by the said John Twomey was witnessed by Colin Cremin of ....

Signed and Sealed by
the said John Murphy
in the presence of:
Brian Swift   John Murphy"

Mortgage by Purchaser to Lender

Where the purchaser is financing the purchase with a loan secured by a legal mortgage, a mortgage must be executed in favour of the mortgagee. This mortgage, like the conveyance from vendor to purchaser, is also almost invariably registered under the Registry of Deeds system.[10]

The forms of mortgages of unregistered land are more or less standardised, and are readily ascertainable by reference to one of the many accepted sources of precedents. Following is a precedent for a mortgage of an unregistered fee simple:–

---

10. If the property is registered land, the mortgage will take the form of a charge on the property. Such a charge, under the Registration on Title Act, 1964, section 69, will not bind the property unless it is registered as a burden on the folio. It may be created, transferred and released by instruments in such one of the Land Registry forms 67 to 72 as may be applicable.

Commencement and Date	"THIS INDENTURE made the ..... day of ..... 19... BETWEEN John Twomey of ..... in the County of Cork, Farmer (hereinafter called the Borrower) of the
Parties	one part and Bank Emerald Ltd. having its registered office at ..... in the County of Cork (hereinafter called the Mortgagee) of the other part.
Recitals of Title	WHEREAS the Borrower is seised of the property hereby mortgaged for an estate in fee simple in possession free from encumbrances.
and of Agreement for loan	AND WHEREAS the Mortgagee has agreed with the Borrower to lend him the sum of £35,000 upon having repayment thereof with interest thereon at the rate hereinafter mentioned secured in the manner hereinafter appearing.
First Testatum Consideration and Receipt Clause	NOW THIS INDENTURE WITNESSETH that in pursuance of the said agreement and in consideration of the sum of £35,000 now paid to the Borrower by the Mortgagee (the receipt whereof the Borrower hereby acknowledges) the
Operative Words	Borrower as beneficial owner hereby grants to the Mortgagee ALL THAT
Parcels	AND THOSE part of the property in the Townland of Rath, Barony of East Carbery, County of Cork, and consisting of four acres and a dwelling house thereon more particularly delineated on the map hereon endorsed and thereon sur-
Habendum	rounded by a red verge line TO HOLD unto and to the use of the Mortgagee in fee simple subject to the proviso for

Proviso for Redemption	redemption hereinafter contained PROVIDED ALWAYS that if the Borrower or his assigns shall on the...... day of ..... next pay to the Mortgagee or its assigns the sum of £35,000 with interest thereon in the meantime at the rate of 12% per annum the Mortgagee or its assigns shall at any time thereafter, at the request and cost of the Borrower or his assigns, reconvey the property hereinbefore granted to the use of the Borrower in fee simple. NOW THIS
Second Testatum Covenants by the Borrower	INDENTURE FURTHER WITNESSETH that the Borrower hereby covenants with the Mortgagee to pay to the Mortgagee on the said ..... day of ..... next, the said sum of £35,000 with interest thereon in the meantime at the rate of 12% per annum from the date of these presents and that the Borrower hereby covenants with the Mortgagee that he will during the continuance of the mortgage keep the property insured against fire up to its full value and will maintain
Powers of Mortgagee	the said property in good and substantial repair AND that if default shall at any time be made by the Borrower or his assigns in complying with any of the aforesaid covenants the Mortgagee or its assigns may enter into possession of the property hereinbefore granted, or appoint a receiver over it, or may sell the said property.
Statutory Certificates	IT IS HEREBY CERTIFIED that the transaction hereby effected does not

form part of a larger transaction or of a series of transactions in respect of which the amount or value or the aggregate amount or value of the consideration exceeds £50,000.

AND IT IS HEREBY FURTHER CERTIFIED that the Mortgagee is a bank appearing in the third schedule of the Central Bank Act, 1942, and as such is a qualified person within the meaning of the Land Act, 1965.

Testimonium and Attestation

IN WITNESS WHEREOF the parties hereto have hereunto set their hands and affixed their seals the day and year first herein written.

SIGNED SEALED
AND DELIVERED
by the said John Twomey
in the presence of:

John O'Brien   John Twomey

PRESENT when the
Common Seal of Bank
Emerald Ltd. was
affixed hereto: Joan Creed

Endorsement of Consent under Family Home Protection Act, 1976

I Helen Twomey being the spouse of the within named John Twomey hereby consent for the purpose of section 3 of the Family Home Protection Act, 1976, to the mortgage of the lands described in the within Indenture of Mortgage to Bank Emerald Ltd. for the within consideration.

SIGNED AND SEALED
by the said Helen Twomey
in the presence of:

Elaine Connell   Helen Twomey."

15

Agency and Conveyancing

CREATION OF AGENCY

Agency is a representative relationship whereby one person, called an agent, may acquire rights and duties on behalf of another person, called the principal. Solicitors, estate agents and auctioneers are the most common types of agents that exercise a role in conveyancing transactions.

Agency may be based on either authority or ratification. Agency can also arise in certain necessity situations. These different means whereby the relationship of principal and agent can be created will be considered in turn.

AGENCY BY AUTHORITY

Express Authority

Express authority is based on consensus. No formality is necessary in the creation of an agency by express authority, except where the agent is authorised to execute a deed – the authority in such a case must normally be given under seal, and is called a power of attorney. Thus, for instance, an agent authorised to execute a deed of conveyance must be empowered to do so by power of attorney.

Implied Authority

Implied authority is that which is reasonably or customarily implied from a larger, more general, grant of express authority; the implied authority will be auxiliary to the express authority. Appointment to a position is a fertile source of implied authority. An agent who has express authority also has implied authority to do all subordinate acts that are incidental to the exercise of his express authority. The extent of the authority implied in any given case will depend on such factors as the trade or business concerned, and any course of dealing that may exist between the parties.

The scope of the implied authority engendered by a position may also involve a question of law.[1]

Apparent Authority   HELLO!

Agency can derive from an authority that may be described either as apparent or ostensible.

Agency arising in this way is based on estoppel. It results from a representation by a principal that causes a third person reasonably to believe that a person, who may or may not be the principal's agent, has authority to enter into negotiations or to make representations as his agent.

This form of agency by authority can apply where the express or implied authority of an agent is subject to a limitation that is unknown to the third person. It can also apply however to a situation where an agent has no authority in relation to a particular transaction, or even where the prior relationship of principal and agent does not exist.

AGENCY BY RATIFICATION

Agency may be based on ratification. This is the affirmation by a person of a prior act that did not bind him but that

---

1. The case of *Law* v. *Roberts and Co. (Ireland) Ltd.* [1964] I.R. 292 established the limits on the implied authority of an estate agent.

was done, or professedly done, on his account.

A ratification may be either express or implied from conduct, and it is unnecessary that it be communicated to the third party.

The doctrine of ratification is invoked primarily in relation to contracts. A ratification, if made within a reasonable time after a contract made by an agent, renders the principal a party to the contract. The ratification operates retrospectively.

The following are the main rules that govern the validity of a ratification. First, the agent must have expressly contracted as agent for a principal who was sufficiently described so as to be identifiable by the third party.[2]

Secondly, the principal must have existed and been competent to make the contract when it was, in fact, made. This requirement formerly precluded the ratification by a company of pre-incorporation contracts. This obstacle to ratification by a company was removed by section 37 of the Companies Act, 1963.

Thirdly, certain transactions are unratifiable. Thus, a void contract is unratifiable, although a voidable contract can be ratified before it has been avoided. Also, a forgery cannot be ratified.

Fourthly, a ratification is not binding unless made by the principal with full knowledge of all material facts.[3]

Finally, ratification of part of a contract is ineffective, since such would impose a new contract on the third party.

---

2. See, e.g., *Keighley, Maxsted and Co.* v. *Durant* [1901] A.C. 240.
3. The case of *Brennan* v. *O'Connell and Another* [1975] Unrep. [Sup. Ct., I.R.] [1974 No. 8] dealt with the information that must be supplied by an estate agent to a vendor in order that a valid ratification take place.

AGENCY OF NECESSITY

An agency of necessity is conferred by common law on a deserted wife, and a similar agency is presumed in favour of a wife who is cohabiting with her husband. Agency of necessity can also be inferred in a commercial setting. These types of agency are rarely relevant in the conveyancing context.

RELATIONSHIP BETWEEN PRINCIPAL AND AGENT

The relationship between a principal and an agent is a fiduciary one. The rights and duties incidental to the relationship depend primarily on the contract, express or implied, between the parties.

The basic duties of an agent are to obey the principal, to exercise diligence and skill, to act personally, to act in good faith and to keep accounts. The basic rights of an agent are to be indemnified for expenses, to obtain a commission and to exercise a lien or stoppage in transit.

DUTIES OF AN AGENT

1. Obedience

An agent must obey the lawful instructions given by his principal. A gratuitous agent may refuse to follow instructions but, in such event, he is normally under a duty to advise the principal of his inactivity.

2. Diligence and Skill

The standard of diligence and skill required of an agent depends on whether the agent is acting for reward or merely gratuitously. An agent who is acting for reward must exercise such diligence and skill as is necessary for the due performance of his undertaking.

A gratuitous agent must exercise only such diligence and skill as he may have, or as he may represent himself as having.

3. Act Personally

The duty of an agent to act personally is expressed in the maxim, "Delegatus non potest delegare".

The duty is not an absolute one, and an agent may frequently delegate performance. Delegation may be authorised either expressly or impliedly, it may be sanctioned by usage or custom, or it may be reasonably necessary to effect the purpose of the agency.[4]

4. Good Faith

An agent owes a duty to his principal to act in good faith.

This duty prohibits the agent from acting contrary to the interests of the principal. Thus, an agent may not mis-use confidential information that is acquired during the course of the agency. This preclusion continues even after the termination of the agency.

The requirement to act in good faith also obliges the agent to surrender any secret profits acquired by virtue of his position. Any profits so made are recoverable by the principal. An agent is entitled to make an incidental profit in the course of the agency, provided that full disclosure is made in advance to the principal.

---

4. See, e.g., *Hedley Byrne and Co. Ltd.* v. *Heller and Partners Ltd.* [1963] 2 All E.R. 575.

5. Accounts

An agent is required to keep accounts of all transactions involving the principal, and must render these on request to the principal.

Such accounts should be kept separate from the personal accounts of the agent. If the accounts are mixed, money that the agent cannot prove to be his own will be presumed to belong to the principal.

The keeping of accounts by certain classes of agents – such as solicitors – is governed by statutory regulations.

RIGHTS OF AN AGENT

1. Indemnity

The contract between a principal and an agent may expressly entitle the agent to be indemnified in respect of any expenses properly incurred in the execution of the agency. Even in the absence of an express provision, the right of an agent to be indemnified will normally be implied by the courts.

2. Commission

(a) Contract Overriding

The right of an agent to a commission depends in the first instance on the contract made with the principal. While there is a considerable diversity of principles pertaining to the entitlement of an agent to a commission, any express terms on the matter will be controlling.

(b) Interpretation of Contract

Even where an express contractual term exists, difficulties on its interpretation can arise. The entitlement of estate agents to commission has been a fertile source of litigation in this respect. For instance, where an agent is retained by a vendor to find a purchaser, it is settled that no entitlement to commission arises until a binding contract is made between the vendor and a purchaser who has been introduced by the agent. A similar interpretation applies where an agent is expressly entitled to commission in the event of business resulting.[5]

Conversely, if an estate agent is retained to introduce a purchaser who is willing and able to purchase, or who is ready and willing to purchase, a court would be more likely to hold that an entitlement to a commission existed even if no contract resulted between the principal and the prospective purchaser. Nevertheless, the mainstream of the litigation in this area requires that, before an estate agent is entitled to commission, a purchaser should have been introduced and, in addition, the purchase should have been completed.[6]

(c) Sole and Exclusive Agents

The designation of an agent as sole or exclusive affects the rights to a commission. A person appointed as sole or exclusive agent to obtain a contract is entitled to remuneration if the contract is obtained by another agent, but is not entitled to remuneration where the contract is obtained by the principal.[7]

A person appointed as sole agent, as exclusive agent, or as sole and exclusive agent, with exclusive rights to sell, is entitled to commission irrespective of who obtains the contract.

---

5. See, e.g., *Murdoch Hownie Ltd.* v. *Newman* [1949] 2 All E.R. 783.
6. See, e.g., *James H. North Ltd.* v. *Dinan* [1931] I.R. 486.
7. See, e.g., *Murphy, Buckley and Keogh Ltd.* v. *Pye (Ireland) Ltd.* [1971] I.R. 57.

(d) Contracts Prohibited by Statute

If an entitlement to a commission is contained in a contract that is prohibited by statute, the commission will be irrecoverable. Thus, an unlicensed house agent who transacts a sale is not entitled to a commission.[8]

(e) Quantum Meruit

In the absence of an express term on the matter, an agent may have an implied right to a commission on a quantum meruit basis. The preconditions to this implied right are that a contract to do work should have been made, and that the work specified should have been carried out. In such event, the agent is entitled to reasonable remuneration for the work performed.[9]

3. Lien

An agent has the right to a lien on the goods of his principal in respect of any claims against the principal, whether such claims relate to commission, to indemnity or to liabilities incurred.

The scope of the lien depends on whether the agent is classifiable as general or particular. A general agent is one appointed to carry out a series of transactions for a principal. Such an agent may exercise a lien, by way of security, on any property of the principal held by him.

A particular agent is one appointed to carry out a single transaction for the principal. His right to a lien extends only to such property as is held by him in connection with that transaction.

---

8. See, e.g., *Somers* v. *Nicholls* [1955] I.R. 83.
9. See, e.g., *Henehan* v. *Courtney* and Hanley, 101 I.L.T.R. 25.

4. *Stoppage in Transit*

An agent may pledge his own credit in respect of goods ordered on behalf of a principal. If payment for the goods is not forthcoming from the principal, the agent may stop the goods in transit.

RELATIONSHIP OF PRINCIPAL AND AGENT TO THIRD PARTIES

It is a basic tenet of the doctrine of agency that the legal relations of a principal with regard to third parties can be altered by means of a contract made by an agent. Such a contract may specify whom – as between the principal, the agent and the third party – will acquire rights and obligations under it. More frequently, however, the agreement will be silent on these matters, and these will then fall for resolution under the common law principles now to be considered.

Principal's Participation in Third Party Contracts

Certain general rules have been developed at common law with regard to the participation by a principal in a contract made by an agent. While the matter depends primarily upon the intention of the parties, it is possible to distinguish in broad terms between the following three situations. The first situation that can be considered is where an agent has authority to make the contract, and where he is known to be an agent. The general rule in this case is that the principal can either sue or be sued on the contract, irrespective of whether or not he had been named. This rule can be displaced by the terms of the contract, whether expressly or by implication.

A second situation that can arise is where the agent has authority to make the contract, but does not disclose the existence of the agency. The doctrine of the undisclosed principal applies here. Under this doctrine either the agent or the principal may sue the other party to the contract and either the agent, or the principal when discovered, may be sued. There are however qualifications. The contract, whether expressly or by implication, may be confined to the parties themselves, and may thus negative the right of the principal to sue on it. The third party moreover, when he has discovered the existence of the principal, must elect to sue either the agent or the principal. The initiation of proceedings against either the agent or the principal is not necessarily conclusive that such an election has been made.

Finally, a third situation that can occur is where an agent, without the authority of the principal, makes a contract with a third party. The principal will normally be neither entitled nor liable on such a contract in the absence of ratification. Liability in tort may however rest with the principal, if the making of the contract had been attended by fraud.[10]

Agent's Participation in Third Party Contracts

The extent to which an agent participates in a contract made by him on behalf of a principal again depends primarily on the intention of parties. The courts, in seeking to ascertain this intention, attach special significance to the degree of disclosure relating to the agency that is made by the agent at the time of contracting – the greater the disclosure that has been made, the lesser is the likelihood that the agent will be held to have pledged personal responsibility on the contract made.

Three situations can be distinguished. The first is where the agent has authority to make the contract, and where he is known to be an agent. An agent, in this situation, normally possesses neither rights nor liabilities with regard to the third party. This general rule may be displaced by the express or implied terms of the contract. Such displacement is more readily inferred where, although the fact of the agency has

---

10. See, e.g., *Lloyd* v. *Grace, Smith & Co.* [1922] A.C. 716.

been disclosed, the identity of the principal has been withheld.

The second situation that can be considered is where the agent – although he has authority to make the contract – does not disclose the existence of the principal. The agent here may enforce the contract. He is also liable on the contract, although the third party, in deciding against whom to enforce the contract, must elect between the principal and the agent.

A third situation that can arise is where a contract made by an agent had not been authorised by the principal. The agent will normally be entitled to enforce such a contract, unless he had purported to represent a named principal. Conversely, the agent can be held liable in contract for breach of an implied warranty of authority. He may also be made liable in tort if the making of the contract had been attended by fraud.[11]

Special Rules Regarding Participation in Third Party Contracts

There are a number of special rules, in addition to the general rules that have been discussed, in relation to the question of who, as between the principal and agent, participates in a contract made by an agent. First, contracts under seal are treated differently. The basic rule is that the agent only, and not the principal, is liable and entitled under such contracts. There are circumstances, however, where a principal may be entitled and liable on a contract under seal made by an agent. These circumstances are where:–

1. the authority to make the contract has been given to the agent by deed,
2. the contract is made by the agent in the presence of the principal, or
3. the agent executes the contract under seal in the capacity of trustee.

---

11. See, e.g., *Polhill v. Walter* [1832] 3 B. and Ad. 114.

Secondly, special rules govern liability on negotiable instruments. Thus, an agent normally incurs no liability on such an instrument unless his name appears on it. Moreover, even should his name appear on it, an agent will normally be exempted from liability on the instrument if a qualification appears which indicates that he is acting in a purely representative capacity. Thirdly, the position of an agent as a contracting party may be determined by a trade usage. Such usage may be incorporated as an implied term in a contract made by an agent.

Miscellaneous Matters arising on Third Party Contracts

Apart from the central question of who is entitled and liable on contracts made by an agent, a number of other issues that bear on the relationship between the principal, the agent and the third party have recurred in litigation. Some of the more important of these issues will now be considered.

1. Payments to Agent

An agent who has received payment from either the principal or third party may fail to pass the money on to the creditor. The question then arises as to whether the person who has made the payment is liable to make a second payment to the creditor. There are two separate situations.

First, the general rule is that a principal is not discharged by paying to an agent money that is owed to a third party. It is irrelevant that the third party was unaware of the agency. An exception to the general rule arises where the third party shows either by words or conduct that he looks to the agent alone for payment. The principal will then be discharged by paying the agent, since the third party will be estopped from requiring a second payment.

Secondly, the question can also arise in the converse

case, namely, where the third party pays the agent and the latter fails to pass the money on to the principal. The general rule here is that the third party is discharged by paying the agent, provided that the agent had authority to receive the money or, alternatively, that the receipt of the money by the agent had subsequently been ratified by the principal.[12]

In the case of *Barclays Bank* v. *Breen* the court noted that a solicitor as such has no implied authority to receive the purchase money for property sold, except on production of a deed duly executed and containing a receipt for the consideration by the person entitled to give a receipt therefor.[13]

2. Set-Off

A third party may be entitled to set-off money owed to him by an agent against money owed by him to the principal. The question can arise where an agent, who owes a personal debt to a third party, is entrusted with possession of goods by a principal. The third party may be entitled to a set-off if he buys the goods from the agent under a genuine belief that the latter is a principal in the transaction. He must prove however that the agent sold the goods in his own name as if they were his own, and also that the set-off had accrued before he became aware of the identity of the real principal in the transaction.

3. Principal Styled as Agent

A somewhat unusual situation can arise where a person, although purporting to be an agent, is in fact the principal. A contract made by a person in these circumstances is enforceable by the third party. Moreover, the principal

---

12. The case of *Barclay's Bank* v. *Breen,* 96 I.L.T.R. 179 illustrates the discharge of a purchaser by payment to the vendor's solicitor.
13. 96 I.L.T.R. 179. See, also, Conveyancing Act, 1881, s. 56.

who has styled himself as agent can also enforce the contract, provided that the supposed principal has not been named and also that the identity of the parties is not material under the contract.

TERMINATION OF AGENCY

An agency may be terminated either by the act of the parties or by operation of law. Third parties can enforce contracts made by the agent prior to the termination, and, in certain circumstances, contracts made by a person whose agency has terminated.

Termination by Act of the Parties

Termination of agency by act of the parties can occur, first, by mutual agreement. Secondly, it will occur if the principal revokes the authority of the agent. The following qualifications exist on the right of a principal to revoke the authority of an agent:—

a. Express Terms

The express terms of the agency agreement may place limitations on the principal's right of revocation. An instance would arise where an agency is given by means of an irrevocable power of attorney.

b. Implied Terms

Where the relationship of principal and agent is akin to that of employer and employee, the principal must give such notice of revocation as is customary and reasonable.[14]

---

14. See, e.g., *Irish Welding Co. Ltd.* v. *Philips Electrical (Ireland) Ltd.* [1976] Unrep. [H.C., R.I.] [1974, No. 3565P].

c. Agency in Progress

A principal can not avoid the payment of commission by revoking an agency where the agent is in the process of completing his work.[15]

d. Agency coupled with Interest

An agency is regarded as coupled with an interest in this context only where the agency is created in order to protect the interest. The restraint on revocation therefore does not apply where the agency existed before the interest.

Termination of agency by act of the parties can arise, thirdly, where the agent renounces the agreement. Such renunciation must be in accordance with any express or implied terms of the agency. Otherwise, the principal will have an action for breach of agreement.

Termination by Operation of Law

Termination of agency by operation of law can occur, first, by complete performance of the contract. This is the normal method of termination. Secondly, expiration of time will terminate an agency created for a fixed period. Thirdly, the death or insanity of either the principal or the agent will determine the relationship.

Fourthly, an agency will be terminated by the bankruptcy of the principal. The bankruptcy of an agent will not automatically have the same effect, although it confers on the principal a right to dismiss the agent if the latter's insolvency renders him unfit to act.

Finally, an agency will be terminated by a supervening illegality or by frustration.

---

15. See, e.g., *Ward and Fegan* v. *Spivack Ltd.* [1957] I.R. 40.

Position of Third Parties on Termination of Agency

A third party who has made a contract with an agent before the termination of the agency is normally both entitled and liable on such contract even after the termination.

Special considerations apply to contracts made by a third party with an agent after the agency has been determined. The general rule is that the principal acquires neither rights nor obligations under such an agreement. Nevertheless, although both the express and implied authority of an agent may have ceased, his apparent authority will bind the principal unless the third party had been notified of the cessation of authority.

The termination of an agency by the death of the principal provides an illustrative framework in which to consider the position of a third party who contracts with a person whose agency has been determined, but whose apparent authority continues. The third party in these circumstances, provided he had been unaware at the time of contracting of the principal's death, can enforce the agreement against the estate of the principal. Moreover, the third party can also sue the agent in contract for breach of an implied warranty of authority.

It has been held that similar rules apply in the event of the termination of agency by reason of the insanity of the principal.

AUCTIONEERS AND ESTATE AGENTS

Auctioneers

An auctioneer is a person employed to sell property by auction. He is primarily an agent for the seller, although he may also act as agent for the buyer for limited purposes, such as the signing of a contract of sale.[16]

Auctioneers are regulated under the Auctioneers and House Agents Acts, 1947, 1967 and 1973. This legislation requires that an auctioneer be licensed, and also that he lodge a deposit in the High Court as one of the conditions of the granting of the licence. In addition, an auctioneer is under a statutory duty to keep an account of his client's money.

The basic duties of an auctioneer at common law are to follow the instructions of the principal, and to exercise reasonable diligence and skill in the performance of his work.[17] Also, an auctioneer should normally act in person, although a limited power of delegation exists.[18]

Having sold a property by auction, an auctioneer has an implied authority to sign the contract of sale on behalf of both the seller and the buyer. The implied authority of an auctioneer to sign on behalf of the buyer is confined to the saleroom and may not extend to his employees.[19]

The conduct of an auction of real property is subject to the Sale of Land by Auction Act, 1867; this provides that a vendor must expressly reserve any right either to set a reserve price or to bid at the auction.

House or Estate Agents

A house agent within the meaning of the Auctioneers and House Agents Acts, 1947, 1967, and 1973, is an agent who, otherwise than by auction, sells, purchases or negotiates for the sale or purchase of any building. Such agents are subject to similar licensing requirements as auctioneers.

---

16. See, e.g., *McMeekin* v. *Stevenson* [1917] I.R. 348.
17. See, e.g., *Kavanagh* v. *Cuthbert* [1874] I.R. 9 C.L. 136.
18. See, e.g., *Dyas* v. *Stafford* [1871] 7 L.R. Ir. 590.
19. See, e.g., *Sheridan* v. *Higgins* [1971] I.R. 291.

The basic duties of a house agent to follow instructions, to exercise diligence and skill and to act personally are also analogous with those of an auctioneer.

The implied authority of a house agent is, in general terms, less extensive than that of an auctioneer. A house agent as such, for instance, has implied authority neither to sell nor to sign a contract on behalf of the principal.[20]

---

20. See, e.g., *Law* v. *Roberts & Co. (Ireland) Ltd.* [1964] I.R. 292.

Part Three

Legislation on Land
and Conveyancing Law

Summary of Part Three

16. Settled Land Acts	203
17. Registration of Deeds	214
18. Registration of Title	220

16

Settled Land Acts

INTRODUCTION

Settlements are arrangements under which property is enjoyed by persons in succession. The modern form of settlement normally arises in the family rather than the commercial context. For instance, a person in his will bequeaths his property to his wife for life, remainder to his children in equal shares as soon as they reach the age of twenty one. The will may also contain an express provision appointing trustees with power to distribute income to the children for their maintenance prior to their reaching the age of twenty one.

The major problem arising in relation to nineteenth century settlements was that they rendered land substantially inalienable. Moreover, the holders of intermediate estates under a settlement might have neither the private means to maintain the property nor the power to dispose of the property in order to raise capital. The result in the case of many settled estates was that the property comprised in them had deteriorated and fallen into disrepair. The Settled Land Acts were passed to meet this situation.[1] The major thrust of these Acts was to confer on limited owners of settled property rights of disposition in respect of the property beyond the extent of their ownership. From the foregoing, it is clear that the legislation was essentially designed to promote good estate management.

---

1. Settled Land Acts, 1882-1890.

SETTLED LAND DEFINED

Settled land is defined as "(Any) land or any estate or interest therein which under any document or documents stands for the time being limited to or in trust for any persons by way of succession."[2] Thus the essentials of a settlement are:-- first, at least one document and, secondly, a succession of interests. The following are instances:-- first, property is given by deed "to James Crowley for life, remainder to John Smith and his heirs"; and secondly, pro-- perty is bequeathed by will "unto and to the use of Kevin Cross in fee simple in trust for Mary Cross for life, remainder in trust for Brian Jones in fee simple."

TENANT FOR LIFE

A tenant for life is defined as including any holder of a limited estate. The legislation gives extended powers of dealing with settled land to limited owners. These limited owners may be life tenants, tenants in tail or tenants in fee simple subject to a grant over. The phrase "tenant for life" is used in the legislation to include, not only those with an actual life estate, but also any other person who has the powers of a tenant for life.[3]

The statutory powers of a tenant for life are fiduciary and can be used only in the interests of the settled estate, and not merely for the personal benefit of a tenant for life.[4] Therefore, the exercise of the statutory powers can be restrained – for instance, where a tenant for life proposes to sell settled property at below market value, or otherwise

---

2. Settled Land Act, 1882, s. 2(3).
3. Settled Land Act, 1882, s. 58(1).
4. Settled Land Act, 1882, s. 53.

to deal with such property in a manner prejudicial to the interests of other beneficiaries under a settlement.[5] A disposition will not be restrained however if it is proper in other respects, notwithstanding that it is motivated by selfishness or even malice.[6]

POWERS OF A TENANT FOR LIFE

The legislation confers on the tenant for life wide powers of sale, exchange, leasing, mortgaging and otherwise dealing with the property. These powers are not assignable and cannot in general be curtailed either directly or indirectly.[7]

1. *Powers of Sale and Exchange*

The tenant for life may sell or exchange the settled land either by auction or private treaty.[8] Any sale must be for the best price that can reasonably be obtained.[9] One month's notice must be given to the trustees of a settlement before any sale or mortgage is effected.[10] The general rule is that the proceeds of sale must be invested under the same trusts as were provided for in the settlement.[11]

2. *Power to Grant Leases*

The legislation also confers a power to grant leases on

---

5. See, eg., *Wheelwright* v. *Walker* [1883] 23 Ch.D. 752.
6. For instance, where the tenant for life is "selling out of ill will or because he does not like the remainderman, or because he desires to be relieved the trouble of attending to management of land or from any other such objective or with any such motive":– *Cardigan* v. *Curzon-Howe* [1885] 30 Ch.D. 531.
7. Settled Land Act, 1882, s. 50.
8. Settled Land Act, 1882, s. 3.
9. Settled Land Act, 1882, s. 4(1).
10. Settled Land Act, 1882, s. 45.
11. Settled Land Act, 1882, s. 20.

the tenant for life.[12] Such leases may be granted only up to certain maximum periods, as follows:–

First, building leases may be granted only for a maximum of ninety nine years. The court may however sanction a lease for a longer period if the land in question is situate in an urban area. In such event, the court may permit a lease for a term of up to one hundred and fifty years.[13]

Secondly, mining leases may be granted only for a maximum of sixty years. A court may however sanction a mining lease for a longer period, if the tenant for life can show that it is difficult to lease for a period of sixty years or less.

Thirdly, leases other than building or mining leases may be granted only for a maximum of thirty five years. If, however, a tenant for life is obliged to grant a new tenancy under the landlord and tenant legislation, such tenancy may be granted for an extended period in accordance with that legislation.

Leases granted by a tenant for life under the statutory powers are subject to the following conditions:–

a. the lease must be by deed and must take effect within twelve months of its execution;

b. it must reserve the best rent that can reasonably be obtained;

c. any lease must contain a covenant by the lessee to pay rent and a re-entry clause in the event of the rent not being paid within a specified time not exceeding thirty days;

---

12. Settled Land Act, 1882, s. 6.
13. A court may allow leases for longer terms than those set out in the legislation if it is difficult to make a lease for a term set out in the Acts. Settled Land Act, 1882, s. 10.

d. a counterpart of the lease must be executed by the lessee and delivered to the tenant for life; and

e. at least one month's notice must be given to the trustees of the settlement.[14]

3. Power to Mortgage

The tenant for life can mortgage his own interest and, under the legislation, has no general power to mortgage beyond the period of that interest. He can however give such mortgages in certain specified circumstances, of which the following are instances:

a. to discharge an incumbrance of a permanent nature on the land, in order to raise money to achieve equality on an exchange or partition of the land;[15] or

b. to satisfy certain claims for compensation arising in respect of the land. For instance, settled property may be a tenement within the meaning of the landlord and tenant legislation. If the property has been tenanted, the tenant on quitting the premises may be entitled to compensation for either disturbance or improvements. In such circumstances, the tenant for life can mortgage the settled property for a period beyond his own interest in order to raise money to meet the claims.[16]

4. Power to Grant Options

A tenant for life may grant options to purchase or lease settled land.[17] The price or rent must be the best reasonably obtainable, and must be fixed when the option is granted.

---

14. Settled Land Act, 1882, s. 7.
15. Settled Land Act, 1882, s. 18.
16. Settled Land Act, 1882, s. 49(2).
17. Settled Land Act, 1882, s. 2.

Any option must be exercisable within an agreed number of years not exceeding ten. Any consideration obtained for the exercise of the option is required to be treated as capital money.

5. *Power to Effect Improvements*

A tenant for life may of course effect improvements at his own expense. In addition, he may be entitled to have the cost of improvements borne out of capital money or raised by a mortgage or charge of the settled land.[18] The works that may be financed by capital money in this way include the construction of, or alterations to, buildings or bridges. Before carrying out such improvements, the tenant for life must submit a detailed scheme of the proposals to either the trustees or the court.[19] The latter are not concerned with the general policy of the scheme, but only with the question of whether the scheme is a proper one within the meaning of the legislation.

TRUSTEES OF THE SETTLEMENT

Identification of the Trustees

The trustees of settled land are identified under the following provisions. First, section 2 of the Settled Land Act, 1882, specifies as trustees any person with a power of sale over the settled land, or any person with a power to consent to or approve such sale. If no person has such

---

18. The works that may be financed by capital money are listed in section 25 of the Settled Land Act, 1882. The list is extended in section 13 of the Settled Land Act, 1890.
19. Settled Land Act, 1882, s. 26. Under section 15 of the Settled Land Act, 1890, the court is given a discretion to authorise expenditure of capital money without the submission of a scheme where it regards it as appropriate.

express power, then the trustees are any persons specifically designated as such by the settlement. Secondly, if the
Act of 1882 is inapplicable, the trustees are identified under
section 16 of the Settled Land Act, 1890. This specifies as
trustees:–

> "(a) the persons, if any, who are for the time being
> under the settlement trustees with power of sale of
> any other land comprised in the settlement and subject
> to the same limitations as the land to be sold or with
> power of consent to, or approval of the exercise of
> such a power of sale, or if there be no such persons,
> then,
> (b) the persons, if any, who are for the time being
> under the settlement trustees with a future trust for
> sale of the land to be sold with power of consent to,
> or approval of, the exercise of such a future power of
> sale and whether the power or trust takes effect in all
> events or not."

Section 16 also provides that, if none of the foregoing
provisions applies, the trustees are any persons so declared
expressly for the purposes of the legislation.

Thirdly, if no trustee exists under the foregoing provisions, an application to the court will generally be necessary
under section 38(1) of the Settled Land Act, 1882, in order
to have an appointment made. An exception exists under
section 50(3) of the Succession Act, 1965. This provides as
follows:–

> "Where land is settled by will and there are no trustees
> of the settlement, the personal representatives prov-
> ing the will, shall, for all purposes, be deemed to be
> trustees of the settlement until trustees of the settle-
> ment are appointed but a sole personal representative

shall not be deemed to be a trustee for purposes of the Settled Land Acts, 1882-1890, until at least one other trustee has been appointed."

Functions of Trustees

The working of the legislation rests almost exclusively with the tenant for life. In general, it can be said that the trustees exercise only limited powers. Thus, their consent to the sale of the mansion house is required under section 10 of the Settled Land Act, 1890.

Trustees, moreover, have certain functions in relation to capital money. Thus, they normally act as depositories of the capital money where no competent person holds the position of tenant for life; for instance, where the tenant for life is an infant, the statutory provisions may be exercised by trustees appointed by the court. The trustees may act as depositories of capital money in other circumstances. For instance, where a tenant for life has disposed of the settled property by sale or otherwise he has the choice of paying the capital money either to the trustees or into court.[20]

The trustees have no general power to direct how capital money shall be reinvested or applied.[21] Moreover, where the capital money is applied in the purchase of land, the trustees have no discretion in making the purchase and are not in any way responsible for the transaction, provided it appears to be within the terms of either the legislation or the settlement.[22]

Where capital money is to be applied for improvements authorised by the legislation, the scheme must be submitted by the tenant for life for the approval of either the

---

20. Settled Land Act, 1882, s. 22.
21. Settled Land Act, 1882, s. 22(2).
22. Settled Land Act, 1882, s. 42.

trustees or the court.[23] Where the trustees have approved the scheme, they are not responsible for payments made under the scheme on receipt of a certificate from a competent engineer or a qualified surveyor. Consequently, the responsibility of the trustees is confined to the approval of the scheme, a matter on which they can obtain professional advice, and thereby practically free themselves from liability.

In dealings between the tenant for life and the settlement, the trustees shall represent and assume the full statutory powers of the tenant for life in respect of the dealing.[24]

Apart from functions conferred by the legislation, the trustees may exercise any functions expressly conferred on them by the settlement. However, where the exercise of such express powers would conflict with statutory powers of the tenant for life, the express powers of the trustees may only be exercised subject to those statutory powers.[25]

OVERREACHING

The concept of overreaching is central to the legislation. The principle is that land subject to a settlement may be disposed of to a purchaser free from the interests under the settlement, even though the purchaser has notice of these interests.[26] The beneficiaries under the settlement are not however defrauded, since they acquire interests in the consideration received for the disposition that correspond to the interests that they had in the land itself. Moreover, their rights are safeguarded in that the consideration received for the disposition, for instance the price on a sale,

---

23. Settled Land Act, 1890, s. 26.
24. Settled Land Act, 1890, s. 12.
25. Settled Land Act, 1882, s. 5.
26. Settled Land Act, 1882, ss. 20, 22 and 40.

or the rent under a lease, is paid either to the trustees or the court as capital money.[27]

The basic provision on overreaching is section 20 of the Settled Land Act, 1882. This states that a statutory disposition by a tenant for life will pass the land, and discharge it from the provisions of the settlement and from all estates, interests and charges to arise thereunder. The above principle is qualified in respect of the following three categories:–

1. Prior Legal Estates

Prior legal estates are any estates, interests or charges that have priority to the settlement. For instance, assume an owner of land mortgages the property. Subsequently, he settles the land on his son for life, with remainder to his grandson in fee simple. The son later sells the fee simple interest under his statutory powers. The purchaser will take the property free from the interests of the grandson, the remainderman under the settlement, but will take it subject to the mortgage that had been created by the settlor prior to the settlement.

2. Certain Legal Mortgages

Dispositions under the statutory powers will not overreach any mortgage or charge that has been created by the tenant for life in order to secure money actually raised at the date of the mortgage deed. For instance, if a tenant for life mortgages settled land in order to effect any improvement, and the mortgagee has actually paid the money, the mortgage cannot be overreached by a subsequent sale under the statutory powers.

---

27. Settled Land Act, 1882, ss. 22 and 46(2).

3. Binding Rights created under the Settlement

Such rights refer to leases, options and other rights that have been created either under the settlement or under the legislation, and that are binding on the successors in title of the tenant for life. For instance, if a tenant for life has made a lease under the legislation, any subsequent sale of the settled property by him will be subject to that lease.

17

Registration of Deeds

INTRODUCTION

The Registry of Deeds system was established by the Registration of Deeds Act, 1707. Its principal functions are as follows. First, it serves to determine priority as between two or more deeds that create conflicting interests affecting the same property. Under the system, priority between the deeds is determined by reference to the dates of their registration.[1] One result of the system therefore is to displace the equitable principles relating to priorities between documents that dispose of unregistered land.[2]

Secondly, the system provides secondary evidence in the event of a loss of title documents, since the memorial that has been registered will contain the main particulars from the deed itself.[3]

There are five distinguishable facets of the Registry of Deeds system. These comprise the documents registrable under the system, the method of registration, the rules governing priority, the records maintained for the system and the process of searching in these records. These facets will be considered in turn.

---

1. Registration of Deeds Act (Ireland), 1707, s. 4.
2. These principles are embodied in the following two maxims. First, "Where the equities are equal, the first in time prevails." Secondly, "Where the equities are equal, the law prevails."
3. Registry of Deeds (Ireland) Act, 1832, s. 32. In the event of lost documents, one may seek secondary evidence in for instance the documents pertaining to adjoining properties, in insurance contracts, as well as in registered memorials.

REGISTRABLE DOCUMENTS

The relevant legislation provides that the following documents may be registered:–

1. any deed or conveyance whereby land or any incorporeal hereditaments are disposed of,
2. a decree of ejectment,
3. a declaration of title, and
4. an order for partition of the property.

The term "conveyance" as used in the Act means any instrument in writing, whether or not under seal, that passes an interest in land from one person to another, regardless of whether the interest is legal or equitable.[4] Thus, for instance, even an agreement for sale may be registered, since this will convey an equitable interest to the purchaser. Certain documents gain nothing by registration, the most important of which is any lease that takes effect in possession and that is for a period of twenty one years or less.[5]

METHOD OF REGISTRATION

The method of registration is governed by sections 6 and 7 of the Act. These provide for registration by the enrolment of a memorial in the Registry of Deeds. A memorial is effectively a summary of the deed that is being registered. The content of memorials is regulated by the legislation. Thus a memorial must contain the following particulars:[6]

---

4. Registration of Deeds Act (Ireland), 1707, ss. 1 and 3.
5. Registration of Deeds Act (Ireland), 1707, s. 14.
6. Registration of Deeds Act (Ireland), 1707, s. 7; and Registry of Deeds (Ireland) Act, 1832, s. 29.

1. the date of execution of the deed,
2. the names and descriptions of all parties and witnesses to the deed, and
3. the description of the property that has been conveyed.

The execution, attestation and proof of a memorial are governed by section 6. This requires that the memorial be executed by one of the grantors or one of the grantees to the deed. The section also provides that the memorial must be attested by two witnesses, one of whom must also have been a witness to the grantor's execution of the deed – the latter is commonly referred to as the "common witness".

An affidavit must be sworn by the witness common to the memorial and the deed. This affidavit is normally contained on the reverse side of the memorial. It will contain verification of the signing and sealing of the memorial, and also of the execution of the deed.[7]

RULES GOVERNING PRIORITIES

The Registration of Deeds Act effectively displaces in most circumstances the equitable rules relating to priority between conflicting instruments that affect the same unregistered property. The following are the main rules set out in the legislation.

1. *Conflict between Registered and Unregistered Deeds*

A registered deed takes priority over an unregistered deed affecting the same property, irrespective of the dates of execution of the deeds.[8]

---

7. A precedent memorial has already been given. See, *supra*, Chapter 14 at pages 178 and 179.
8. Registration of Deeds Act (Ireland), 1707, s. 5.

2. Conflict between Registered Deeds as between Themselves

The priority as between two or more registered deeds is determined by the dates of registration of the deeds.[9] This rule may be displaced by the doctrine of notice provided for in the legislation; under this doctrine a party affected with actual or imputed notice of a previous unregistered instrument cannot rely in equity on the statutory priority.

3. Conflict between Registered Deeds where one of them is Voluntary

The registration of a voluntary deed confers no priority over a prior unregistered deed so long as none but volunteers claim under the voluntary deed.[10]

4. Conflict between Unregistered or Unregistrable Deeds

The Act has no application in conflicts between deeds that have not been registered, or between deeds that are not registrable.[11] Priority in such circumstances is governed by the principles of equity that govern priority.

RECORDS MAINTAINED IN THE REGISTRY OF DEEDS

The following records are kept. First, a Day Book is used to record the time of receipt of memorials. Secondly, an Abstract Book is used to maintain particulars of the memorials that have been enrolled. Thirdly, a Transcript Book is kept in which memorials are fully set out.

---

9. Registration of Deeds Act (Ireland), 1707, s. 4.
10. See, e.g., *Re Flood's Estate* [1862] 13 Ir.Ch.R. 312.
11. Registration of Deeds Act (Ireland), 1707, ss. 5 and 14.

Fourthly, an Index of Names is maintained that contains the names of the grantors as set out in the memorials that have been enrolled. In practice, it is the most important record maintained by the Registry, since a purchaser of property will normally require a search against all parties appearing on the title in respect of the period for which such a search is appropriate.

SEARCHES IN THE REGISTRY OF DEEDS

Types of Search

There are two principal types of search in the Registry of Deeds, namely, unofficial and official searches. Unofficial searches are commonly referred to as hand searches, and they may be made by any member of the public on paying the prescribed fee.[12] In practice, however, these searches are normally made by professional law searchers.

Official searches in the Registry of Deeds are of two types, namely, common searches and negative searches.[13] A common search is made by one official of the Registry and is initialled on behalf of the Registrar. The Registry does not accept liability for errors contained in the result of a common search. The second type of official search is the negative search: this is made by two officials of the Registry and the Registry accepts responsibility for any errors in the results given in respect of such a search.

In practice, the most usual search adopted is a negative search in the Index of Names against all parties on the title. A hand search may also be used to complement the negative search, where the negative search has not been made to include the full period up to the closing of a transaction.

---

12. Registry of Deeds (Ireland) Act, 1832, s. 29.
13. Registration of Deeds Act (Ireland), 1707, s. 8; and Registry of Deeds (Ireland) Act, 1832, s. 29.

The Period of Search

The general rule is that one searches against the parties on the title from the date on which they acquired an interest in the property to the date of registration of the deed by which they disposed of the property. A party generally acquires an interest in property from the date on which that party signs a contract to purchase the property. The purchaser at that point acquires an estate interest, which is an equitable interest in the property. In practice, one will generally not be aware of the date on which a party on the title signed the contract of sale; therefore, the normal practice is to commence the search from the date of the deed by which the party acquired the interest.

If a deed has been executed, but not registered, then one searches from the date of the deed to the present day.

There are special rules relating to the searches that must be made in the event of a death on the title. One searches against the beneficiary from the date of death, since he is entitled to deal with the property from that date. Although he would not be entitled to pass a legal interest in the estate pending the grant of representation and assent from the personal representative he could, for instance, mortgage the inheritance. One also searches against the personal representatives from the date of death. The search will be made to the present day, if there has been a sale in the course of administration. Alternatively, if the personal representatives have vested the property in the beneficiaries, one searches until the date of registration of the assent from the personal representatives.

One also searches against the deceased. The search is made from the date on which he acquired an interest in the property until six months after his death, since a deed executed by him before death might not be registered until some time after his death.

18

Registration of Title

INTRODUCTION

The system of registration of title had two principal objects when first introduced on an extensive scale by the Local Registration of Title (Ir.) Act, 1891. The first was to simplify conveyancing. This was achieved in a number of ways. Thus, the legislation introduced the general principle that registration should be conclusive evidence of ownership and title. Important exceptions to this principle have however been introduced in the meantime, and there are a number of instances where an owner or purchaser of registered land can be affected by unregistered rights.[1] The legislation also sought to simplify conveyancing by making land transferable in much the same way as shares in a company. Thus, the basic procedure in the conveyancing of registered land involves the execution of a Land Registry transfer by the transferor and transferee. The executed transfer is then lodged in the Land Registry.

The second objective of the registration of title system was to protect public funds. Under the Land Purchase Acts introduced in the nineteenth century,[2] the holders of agricultural land were given the right to convert their interests from leasehold to freehold, and so reverse the pattern established by the plantations and the Penal Laws.

---

1. See, e.g., Registration of Title Act, 1964, s. 72.
2. Land Purchase Acts, 1860-1901.

Moreover, the government, through the body that eventually became the Irish Land Commission, extended loans to enable the conversion of titles. The government therefore had an interest in ensuring that those who availed of the Land Purchase Acts obtained good title. The system of registration of title served this interest by ensuring that a public register of ownership would be available.

The modern legislation that governs the system is the Registration of Title Act, 1964.

LAND REGISTRY OFFICES AND REGISTERS

Land Registry Offices

The legislation provides for a Central Land Registry Office and also for Local Offices in each county. Ultimate responsibility for the system is given to the Registrar of Titles, although certain responsibilities are also given to the County Registrars.

Section 7 deals with the Land Registry:–

"(1) There shall be a central office in the county borough of Dublin (in this Act referred to as "the central office") and a local office in each county other than Dublin (in this Act referred to as a "local office").

(2) The central office shall be the office for registration of all land in the State.

(3) The functions of the local offices shall be such as may be prescribed.

(4) The central office and local offices shall collectively be known as the Land Registry."

Section 9 deals with the Registering Authorities. This provides in part as follows:

"(1) The central office shall be under the management and control of an officer who shall be called the Registrar of Titles.

(2) The Registrar of Titles shall be appointed by the Government and shall hold office at the pleasure of the Government.

(3) No person shall be appointed to be Registrar of Titles unless at the time of his appointment he is either a barrister-at-law or a solicitor who has practised his profession for not less than ten years.

(4) For the purpose of section (3), service by a barrister-at-law or a solicitor in a situation in the Civil Service shall be deemed to be practice of his profession."

Section 10 deals with the local offices; it provides in part as follows:–

"(1) Subject to the direction and control of the Registrar, every local office shall be under the management of the county registrar of the county in which the local office is situate, and the business of the local office shall be transacted in the Circuit Court office in and for that county.

(2) Every county registrar (other than the county registrar for the county borough and county of Dublin) shall be a local registrar. . ."

Registers

Three registers are maintained in the Central Office,[3] namely, registers of freehold, leasehold and subsidiary interests.

The registers are divided into folios, and a separate folio is opened for each registered holding. Folios are in turn divided into the following three parts. First, there is a description of the property by reference to a Land Registry map. This part also contains details of easements and

---

3. Registration of Title Act, 1964, s. 8.

benefits attaching to the property, as well as a statement of whether or not the property carries mineral rights. In addition, there will be a statement as to whether or not the land certificate has been issued.

The second part of a folio contains a description of the registered owner, and also of the classes of ownership and title that he has. It also gives an account of the devolution of the property. Finally, it contains a note of any cautions or inhibitions that have been registered in respect of the property.

The third part of a folio contains a description of any burdens that affect the registered holding: for instance, it may refer to any mortgages subsisting against the property; it may also state whether the property is subject to any restrictions contained in sections 12 and 45 of the Land Act, 1965.

A folio may also contain a Land Registry map. The map will delineate such matters as rights of way, public roads and the boundaries of the property relative to adjoining property.

A folio requires to be distinguished from a land certificate. A folio is a document of record maintained in the Land Registry, whereas a land certificate is an actual title document.

It is possible to get a certified copy of any registered folio. Such a copy however is evidence of the state of the folio only at the date of issue. Consequently, when acquiring registered property, one should insist on obtaining sight of an up to date copy of the folio.

CLASSES OF OWNERSHIP IN THE LAND REGISTRY

There are two classes of ownership that may be registered for both freehold and leasehold property, namely, full ownership and limited ownership.[4] In the case of freehold property, a person registered as full owner is the person entitled to the fee simple. In the case of leasehold property, the person registered as full owner is entitled to the leasehold interest in possession.

Conversely, in relation to either freehold or leasehold property, a person registered as limited owner will either be a tenant for life or a person with the powers of a tenant for life under the Settled Land Acts.[5]

CLASSES OF TITLE THAT MAY BE REGISTERED

Three Classes of Freehold Title

A person registered as owner of freehold property can be registered with any of three categories of title, namely, absolute, qualified or possessory.[6] The effect of registration with an absolute title is described in section 37(1) which provides as follows:–

> "On registration of a person as full owner of freehold land with an absolute title, an estate in fee simple of the land together with all implied or express rights, privileges, and appurtenances belonging to or appurtentant thereto shall vest in the person so registered."[7]

Stated alternatively, registration as full owner of freehold property with an absolute title confers a fee simple with all the easements, profits and other interests attached to the property.

---

4. Registration of Title Act, 1964, s. 27.
5. Registration of Title Act, 1964, s. 27(b).
6. Registration of Title Act, 1964, s. 37.
7. Certain qualifications are contained in the Registration of Title Act, 1964, s. 37(2) and (3).

The effect of registration of freehold property with a qualified title is described in section 39 as follows:–

"The registration of a person as first registered full or limited owner of freehold land with a qualified title shall have the same effect as registration with an absolute title save that registration of a qualified title shall not affect or prejudice the enforcement of any right appearing by the register to be excepted."

Instances of rights that may be excepted within the meaning of section 39 include annuities, rights of way and rights in respect of part of the property, such as the right of an adjoining owner to an exclusive right of way.

The effect of registration of freehold property with a possessory title is described in section 38(1) as follows:–

"The registration of a person as first registered full or limited owner of freehold land with a possessory title shall not affect or prejudice the enforcement of any rights adverse to or in derogation of the title of that person and subsisting or capable of arising at the time of registration but save as aforesaid shall have the same effect as registration with an absolute title."

Possessory title as defined in the Registration of Title Act, 1964, is the equivalent of a title registered subject to equities under the previous legislation.

Four Classes of Leasehold Title

There are four classes of title that may be registered in respect of leasehold property, namely, absolute, qualified, possessory and good leasehold.[8]

---

8. Registration of Title Act, 1964, s. 40.

Absolute leasehold title is defined as follows:–

"The applicant shall be registered as owner with an absolute title where the title both to the leasehold interest and to the freehold estate and to any intermediate leasehold interest that may exist is approved by the Registrar."[9]

The effect of registration of a qualified leasehold title is stated in section 40(6) as follows:–

"If on an application for registration with an absolute title or a good leasehold title it appears to the Registrar that the title either of the lessor to the reversion or of the lessee to the leasehold interest can be established only for a limited period or only subject to certain reservations, the Registrar may make an entry in the Register excepting from the effect of registration any right."

The effect of registration of a possessory leasehold title is stated in section 40(5) as follows:–

"If the Registrar is not satisfied that the grant of an absolute, good leasehold or qualified title would be warranted he may register the applicant as owner with a possessory title."

Finally, the effect of registration of a good leasehold title is stated in section 40(5) as follows:–

"The applicant shall be registered as owner with a good leasehold title where the title to the leasehold interest is approved by the Registrar."

---

9. Registration of Title Act, 1964, s. 44.

Conversion of Title

The registered owner of property with either a qualified, possessory or good leasehold title may seek to convert the title into an absolute title. The Registrar of Titles has a general discretion to convert a title on his own initiative.[10] In addition, on an application for the registration of a transfer for value of land registered with a possessory title, not being land purchased under the Land Purchase Acts, the applicant must lodge all documents in his possession in relation to the land.[11] The purpose of this provision is to enable the Registrar to decide whether or not to convert the title.

CONCLUSIVENESS OF THE REGISTER

Section 31 of the Registration of Title Act, 1964, provides that the register is conclusive evidence of the title of the owner to the land and of any rights, privileges, or burdens attaching thereto. A former Registrar of Titles has described section 31 as:– "An attempt by the legislature to build up the Iron Curtain of the Register behind which it is not necessary to penetrate".[12] The general principle of the conclusiveness of the register is however subject to several qualifications, of which the following are the more important. First, under section 31, a court may on the grounds of actual fraud or mistake direct the register to be amended. Secondly, under section 32, rectification of the register can be ordered by a court where an error, mis-statement, mis-description or omission has occurred. Apart from this, merely clerical errors can be rectified by the Registrar without

---

10. Registration of Title Act, 1964, s. 50(1).
11. Registration of Title Act, 1964, s. 50(2)(a) and (b).
12. McAllister, *Registration of Title*, (1973) at 277.

resorting to the court. Thirdly, the register may be rectifed on the grounds of adverse possession; this is the most common basis for rectification.[13]

Fourthly, an exception to the principle of conclusiveness is contained in section 72 of the Act. There are numerous burdens contained in section 72. Some of the more important of these include:– death duties, public rights, easements and profits unless they are created expressly after the first registration, and rights acquired or in the course of being acquired under the Statute of Limitations, 1957.

Section 72 constitutes the most important exception to the principle of conclusiveness. In practice, therefore, a purchaser of registered property should insist on a section 72 declaration from the vendor. This declaration will be to the effect that the vendor is unaware of any section 72 burdens affecting the property.

A fifth exception arises in the case of volunteers. A person acquiring registered land by way of gift is in a less advantageous position than a purchaser. A volunteer will take the property subject to the section 69 burdens that are registered, and also to section 72 burdens. In addition, however, he will take the property subject to other unregistered rights. Such rights could include, for instance, the right of beneficiaries under a trust. These rights would not be registered, by virtue of section 92. This provides in subsection one that:–

> "Subject to the provisions of this Act, notice of a trust shall not be entered in the register."

COMPULSORY REGISTRATION

The intention under the 1964 Act was to make registration compulsory throughout the country. Section 23 provides

---

13. Prior to 1964, some 500 applications were made annually for rectification on this basis.

that one must register in certain situations. Freehold property must be registered where the property is acquired under the Land Purchase Acts or under the Labourers Acts, or where property is acquired after January, 1967, by a statutory authority.[14] Freehold property must also be registered in any case to which section 24(2) applies.

Leasehold property must be registered where it is acquired by a statutory authority or where section 24(2) applies.

Regardless of whether the property is freehold or leasehold, there is no compulsory registration for an estate or interest in reversion or remainder; expressed alternatively, future interests need not be registered.

Section 24 is the provision whereby the registration system is to be extended. It provides that the Minister for Justice may by order under section 24(2) provide that compulsory registration will apply to any county or county borough. Where section 24(2) applies, the registration of ownership will become compulsory in the case of freeholds upon conveyance on sale, and in the case of leaseholds upon the grant or assignment on sale of such an interest. The Minister has made an order under section 24(2) that provides for compulsory registration in Laois, Meath and Carlow.[15]

Where registration is compulsory, a transferee will not acquire any interest in the land unless he registers the conveyance to himself within six months of the date of the conveyance, grant or assignment.[16] On registration, however, the transferee's title relates back to the date of execution of the instrument of disposition.

---

14. A statutory authority means a Minister of State, the Land Commission, the Board of Public Works, any local or public authority, and any other body established by direction of any statute.
15. Statutory Instrument Number 87 of 1969.
16. Registration of Title Act, 1964, s. 25.

FIRST REGISTRATION

The general principle on an application for first registration is that the Registrar cannot call for a title in excess of that which may be required under an open contract for the sale of unregistered property.[17] The general principle therefore is that one must produce title for a period of at least forty years, commencing in a good root of title. Important modifications to the general principle have been introduced by virtue of Rule 19 as amended by Statutory Instrument number 89 of 1977. The first paragraph in the revised rule is as follows:–

"Save as aforesaid and as otherwise provided in this rule, the title to be shown by the applicant may commence with a disposition of the property made not less than thirty years prior to the date of the application that would be a good root of title on a sale under a contract limiting only the length of title to be shown."

Apart from this reduction of the period of title required from forty to thirty years, the period of title required may be even less where the market value of the property is less than £25,000. In these circumstances, an applicant may be required to produce title for as little as twelve years where the application is accompanied by a certificate of title from a solicitor.

LAND REGISTRY TRANSFERS

A Land Registry transfer takes the place of a deed of conveyance, assignment or sub-lease in relation to unregis-

---

17.   First registration is governed by Rules 14 to 19 of the Land Registration Rules, 1972, as amended by Statutory Instrument Number 89 of 1977.

tered property. The form of land registry transfer is pre-scribed by the Land Registration Rules.[18] Following is a pre-cedent:–

LAND REGISTRY
TRANSFER

County.......... Folio..........

Transfer dated the .... day of .... 19..... John Murphy, the registered owner in consideration of the natural love and affection which he bears for his wife Mary Murphy hereby transfers the property contained in Folio 4321L of the Register County .... to the said John Murphy and Mary Murphy for all the residue now unexpired of the term of ninety nine years from the .... day of .... 19..... granted by Indenture of Lease dated the .... day of .... 19..... and made between Michael Smith of the one part and John Murphy of the other part. The address of John Murphy and Mary Murphy, in the State for service of notices and their descriptions are: Seaview, Westbay, County ...., Company director and housewife respec-tively. It is hereby certified, etc.

CAUTIONS AND INHIBITIONS

Cautions and inhibitions are means of protecting unre-gistered interests in registered property. A caution is a delaying device requiring that the Registrar must notify the cautioner of any proposed dealing on the folio in respect

---

18. Rule 69 of the Land Registration Rules, 1972.

of which the caution is registered.[19] Cautions are principally used to protect rights arising out of contractual or trustee relationships. The following are instances. First, a person who has contracted to purchase registered property can lodge a caution to prevent the vendor from reselling the property prior to the completion of the sale in favour of the first purchaser. Secondly, the beneficiaries under a trust may lodge a caution to prevent the trustees from dealing with the land subject to the trust in derogation of their beneficial interest.

An inhibition is a similar though stronger device than a caution.[20] The registration of an inhibition precludes any transaction with the affected property. Any person with an unregistered interest in respect of registered property may apply for the entry of an inhibition in respect of the property. Such an entry could inhibit any dealing with the property for a specified period, or until the occurence of a specific event, or until the consent of the person who has filed the inhibition is obtained.

Because an inhibition is used as a specific restriction on dealings, it is the proper device to protect rights that may not mature for several years. The following are instances. First, a person who has obtained an option to purchase registered property within a specified period can enter an inhibition against any dealing with the property during that period. Secondly, an infant beneficiary under a trust, whose interest may not mature until he reaches his maturity, may enter an inhibition in respect of the property for the intervening years. Thirdly, a person who has acquired a future interest by purchase may enter an inhibition against any dealing with the property on the determination of the particular estate.

---

19. Registration of Title Act, 1964, ss. 96 and 97.
20. Registration of Title Act, 1964, s. 20.

LAND REGISTRY SEARCHES

There are two types of Land Registry search, namely, the official search and the priority search.

An official search will disclose the burdens if any registered in respect of the property involved.[21] A priority search goes further and confers on the person making the search certain rights in respect of the folio involved for a period of fourteen days.[22] A priority search is available to a person who has contracted to purchase registered land, or to take a lease of such land, or to lend money on the security of such land. The effect of a priority search is given in section 108 as follows:–

"(1) Where the Registrar is satisfied that the person to whom the certificate of the result of an official search is issued has entered into a contract to purchase, take a lease of, or lend money on the security of a charge on, the land to which the certificate relates, the Registrar shall, at the request of that person, make an entry in the register in the prescribed form.

(2) In any such case, an application for registration of the instrument to complete the contract shall, provided the application is in order and is delivered at the central office within a period of fourteen days after the date of issue of the certificate, rank in priority before any other application for registration made in respect of the land within that period."

A priority search provides absolute protection during its currency. Absent such a search – or a caution or inhibition – a purchaser for value may by registration secure good title against the holder of unregistered rights.

---

21. Registration of Title Act, 1964, s. 107.
22. Registration of Title Act, 1964, s. 108.

LAND CERTIFICATE

The registered owner of property is entitled to possession of a land certificate. Such a certificate is a document of title. It is prima facie evidence of the facts appearing on it as of the date of its issue.

Rule 162 of the Land Registration Rules, 1972, sets out the circumstances in which the land certificate must be produced on an application for the registration of a dealing with registered property. These include dealings:–

1. by the registered owner,
2. with the consent of the registered owner, or
3. by the personal representatives of the registered owner.

The practical importance of the land certificate therefore derives from the fact that its production is required in respect of most dealings with registered property. There are however two types of dealings on the register that do not require production of the land certificate. First, it is not required on the registration of a judgement mortgage. A creditor may convert his judgement debt into a judgement mortgage, and does not need custody or possession of the land certificate in order to register the judgement.

Secondly, applications under section 49 of the Registration of Title Act, 1964, for registration of a title claimed to be acquired under the Statute of Limitations, 1957, do not require production of the land certificate.

Apart from its importance in relation to dealings on the register, land certificates are also commonly used in the creation of equitable mortgages or liens over registered property. Thus, for instance, the holder of a land certificate can deposit it as security for a loan.

Part Four

Appendices on Land
and Conveyancing Law

Summary of Part Four

Appendix A: Stamp Duty   237
Appendix B: Subsidiary Searches in Conveyancing   242
Appendix C: Impact of the Family Home Protection
                       Act, 1976, and the Family Law Act, 1981   245

Appendix A

Stamp Duty

INTRODUCTION

The legislation on stamp duty is contained in the Stamp Act, 1891, and in subsequent Finance Acts. Stamp duty is chargeable on certain instruments. To denote that the duty has been paid, stamps are impressed on or affixed to the instruments.

Stamp duty may be based on the value of a transaction, in which event it is termed ad valorem duty. Alternatively, the duty may be fixed regardless of the value of the transaction.

AD VALOREM DUTY

Ad Valorem Duty on Conveyance or Transfer on Sale

Following are the rates of duty on the conveyance or transfer on sale of property other than stocks or marketable securities:-

CONVEYANCES/TRANSFERS/ASSIGNMENTS of lands, buildings, etc.		
CONSIDERATION/VALUE		DUTY
EXCEEDING	NOT EXCEEDING	
	5,000	Nil
5,000	10,000	1%
10,000	15,000	2%
15,000	25,000	3%
25,000	50,000	4%
50,000	60,000	5%
60,000		6%

When applying the rates in the foregoing Table, the consideration/value is to be rounded up to the next multiple of £100.

Voluntary Dispositions Inter Vivos *Between Living Persons.*

These are liable to the same rate of duty as conveyances or transfers on sale, with the substitution of the market value of the property in place of the consideration on a sale.

Several anti-avoidance provisions are contained in the legislation. For instance, section 47 of the Finance Act, 1981, deems certain conveyances involving sub-purchasers to be voluntary dispositions inter vivos, thus rendering them liable to duty on the value of the property conveyed.

In addition, statutory instrument number 151 of 1985 contains anti-avoidance provisions in relation to the stamp duty chargeable on certain instruments. The instruments affected are:-

(i) A conveyance or transfer on sale where the vendor of the property enters into an agreement for a long lease, or grants rights in relation to the property.

(ii) An instrument that evidences the surrender of a leasehold interest, or the merger of a leasehold interest in a superior interest.

(iii) A declaration by deed to the effect that a term in land is enlarged in a case where the term was created by an instrument executed within six years of the date of the execution of the deed.

Transactions between Related Persons

The duty payable with regard to instruments on transactions between related persons is restricted to 50 per centum of the duty that would otherwise be payable. A person is related to another if he is his lineal descendant, parent, grandparent, step parent, husband, wife, brother or sister of a parent or brother or sister, or lineal descendant of a parent, husband or wife or brother or sister.

Transfers between Associated Companies

Since 1990, there is a relief from transfer stamp duty in the case of reconstructions or amalgamations of certain companies. The relief is available in respect of the acquisition in whole or in part of the undertaking of a company in the context of a *bona fide* reconstruction or amalgamation.

Leases

Ad valorem duty is payable on the granting of a lease on the amount of the consideration, other than rent, moving to the lessor. The rates are similar to those charged under the head of charge "conveyance or transfer on the sale of any property other than stocks or marketable securities". Duty is also payable on that part of the consideration that consists of rent, and rates of duty in this case depend on the length of the term of the lease in question. Under section 75 of the Stamp Act, 1891, an agreement for a lease for any term not exceeding 35 years is to be charged the same duty as if it were an actual lease made for the term and consideration mentioned in the agreement.

Mortgages, Bonds, Debentures and Convenants

Following are the rates of duty applicable to the above documents:

(a) Being the only or principal or primary security (other than an equitable mortgage) for the repayment of money:-

    up to £20,000 - Exempt

    over £20,000 - 0.1%, limited to a maximum duty of £500

(b) Being an equitable mortgage
Amount secured up to £20,000   Exempt
Amount secured over £20,000   50pence per £1,000 or
part of £1,000

(c) Transfer, assignnient or disposition of any mortgage, bond, debenture or covenant (except of a marketable security)
Amount secured up to £20,000   Exempt
Amount secured over £20,000   50pence per £1,000 or
part of £1,000

Chattels

The property in chattels - for instance, trade plant and machinery (other than fixed plant and machinery), motor vehicles, cash, bank balances - generally passes by delivery without documentation. Accordingly, no liability to stamp duty arises. If, however, the chattels form part of a larger transaction with other property that is liable to duty on a conveyance, it is aggregated with the other property for the purpose of determining the rate of duty that applies to the conveyance of that other property. If the chattels are included in the conveyance, they are liable to stamp duty. Under Section 59 of the Stamp Act, 1891, certain chattels are liable to stamp duty at contract stage if included in a contract for sale.

Settlements

Any instrument whereby certain property is settled or agreed to be settled attracts duty at 25p for every £100 or fractional part of £100 of property involved.

FIXED RATE OF DUTY

The following documentary transactions are ones to which a fixed rate of duty of £10 applies:- appointment of a new trustee; declaration of trust; revocation of trust; agreements, deeds and bonds not otherwise specifically charged; conveyance or transfer not specifically charged; duplicate or counterpart of any instrument; and a surrender of any property, not chargeable with duty as a conveyance on sale or as a mortgage.

GENERAL EXEMPTIONS FROM STAMP DUTY

The following are two important categories of transactions that are exempt from stamp duty:

(i) conveyances, transfers or leases of land and houses for charitable purposes in Ireland to bodies or persons or trusts that have been established for charitable purposes only; and
(ii) the creation of a joint tenancy in the family home under section 14 of the Family Home Protection Act, 1976.

Appendix B

Subsidiary Searches in Conveyancing Transactions

INTRODUCTION

It has already been noted that good conveyancing practice requires that negative, common or hand searches be made in transactions relating to unregistered property, and that official or priority searches be made in dealings relating to registered property. These searches constitute an essential part of the formal investigation of title. In addition to the foregoing searches, good conveyancing practice also requires that a number of subsidiary searches be made relating to aspects of the transaction apart from the title aspect. Following is an account of these searches.

FREEHOLD PROPERTY

The following subsidiary searches should be made in respect of freehold property.

1. *Bankruptcy Search*

Such a search should be made in the Bankruptcy Office to ensure that the vendor is not involved in bankruptcy proceedings.

2. *Lis Pendens Search*

Such a search should be made retrospective for a five

year period in the Lis Pendens Register to ascertain whether any litigation is pending against the vendor. For instance, if the vendor is subject to proceedings for the recovery of a debt, the possibility will exist that any judgement given will be converted into a judgement mortgage affecting the vendor's property, including that property which the purchaser is acquiring.

3. Search on the Judgements Register

If a creditor has obtained a judgement against a vendor, then, if it is not satisfied, the creditor may have certain rights over the property in sale. The reasons for this search are similar to those for the search in the Lis Pendens Register.

4. Planning Search

Such a search is critical having regard to the Local Government (Planning and Development) Act, 1963, as amended. Planning authorities have a general obligation to draw up a development plan, that is required to be revised every five years. The development plan is one aspect with which a purchaser may be concerned.

The second aspect that a purchaser should be concerned with is a record of the details of the proceedings and applications in regard to the property being purchased – for instance, particulars of planning applications, appeals and results.

LEASEHOLD PROPERTY

Sheriffs Office Search

In addition to the foregoing searches, a Sheriffs Office search should also be made in respect of leasehold property. The reason is that any execution order against the vendor will affect the leasehold property of the vendor. Such execution order could include, for instance, an order of fieri facias. Leasehold property is a hybrid between real and personal property. If a person is sued for a debt, and the debt is not satisfied, the sheriff may be ordered to seize such property as will satisfy the judgement – as leasehold property is a chattel real, it comes within the type of property that may be affected by an execution order.

SUBSIDIARY SEARCHES FOR BOTH FREEHOLD AND LEASEHOLD PROPERTY

The following subsidiary searches may also require to be made when appropriate.

1. A Companies' Office Search

Such a search should be made when the vendor is a company. A company may be in liquidation or receivership – a notice to this effect would be filed in the Companies Office. A Companies' Office search will also ascertain whether or not the property is security for a debenture issued by the company.

2. Search of Friendly Societies Register

If the vendor is a friendly society, then one should search the Register to ascertain whether or not the society is in the process of being dissolved, or whether the society has been struck off the Register.

3. District Court Office Search

If the property involved is a licensed premises, then a search should be made in the District Court Office to ascertain whether any indorsements exist on the licence attaching to the premises.

Appendix C

Impact of the Family Home Protection Act, 1976, and the Family Law Act, 1981

FAMILY HOME PROTECTION ACT, 1976

Definitions

One of the most important definitions in the Family Home Protection Act, 1976, is that of a "conveyance". This is defined in section 1 as including a mortgage, lease, assent, transfer, disclaimer, release, and any other disposition of property otherwise than by will or donatio mortis causa. The definition also includes an enforceable agreement to make such a conveyance. The latter is important in conveyancing practice, since it means that the consent of the spouse as required by section 3(1) must be given in the contract of sale. Once given in the contract the consent need not be repeated in the conveyance, although in practice it almost invariably is.

The definition of "family home" is given in section 2. This means primarily a dwelling in which a married couple ordinarily reside, or a dwelling where a deserted spouse resides, or a dwelling where a spouse who has been constructively deserted by her husband ordinarily resided.

Certain Conveyances Void

Section 3(1) provides that where a spouse, without the prior consent of the other spouse, purports to convey any

245

interest in the family home to any person except the other spouse then, subject to Section 3(2), (3), and (4), the purported conveyance shall be void.

Exceptions to the Rule in Section 3(1).

The following conveyances are exceptions to the rule that a conveyance contrary to section 3(1) is void:–

1. A conveyance by one spouse to the other.
2. A conveyance made in pursuance of an enforceable agreement made before the marriage of the spouse.
3. A conveyance made to a purchaser for full value who acts in good faith.
4. A sale by a mortgagee under its power of sale under a mortgage deed or under statute.
5. A fifth exception refers to where a spouse without the consent of the other spouse conveys in pursuance of an enforceable agreement made before marriage, or conveys to a purchaser for full value, and that person in turn makes a voluntary disposition of the property. The ultimate transferee receives the protection given to the first purchaser notwithstanding that he himself would not come within one of the exceptions under section 3(1).

Conveyancing Practice

The Family Home Protection Act, 1976, effectively gives each spouse an interest in the family home, and thus restricts the other spouse from disposing of it unilaterally.

The legislation impacts on the conveyancing of residential property at the contract, requisitions and deed stages. When the legislation is applicable, the consent of the spouse who is not the vendor requires to be endorsed on the contract of sale. Also, requisitions are invariably raised regarding the implications, if any, of the legislation in all transactions of residential property. Finally, when the legislation does apply in a transaction, the consent of the non-vendor spouse requires to be endorsed on the conveyance.

FAMILY LAW ACT, 1981

Relevant Provisions

The provisions of this Act of most obvious relevance to conveyancing transactions are sections 3,4 and 5. These read as follows:–

"3.–Where two persons have agreed to marry one another and any property is given as a wedding gift to either or both of them by any other person, it shall be presumed, in the absence of evidence to the contrary, that the property so given was given –

(a) to both of them as joint owners, and

(b) subject to the condition that it should be returned at the request of the donor or his personal representative if the marriage for whatever reason does not take place.

4.–Where a party to an agreement to marry makes a gift of property (including an engagement ring) to the other party, it shall be presumed, in the absence of evidence to the contrary, that the gift –

(a) was given subject to the condition that it should be returned at the request of the donor or his personal representative if the marriage does not take place for any reason other than the death of the donor, or

(b) was given unconditionally, if the marriage does not take place on account of the death of the donor.

5(1) –Where an agreement to marry is terminated, the rules of law relating to the rights of spouses in relation to property in which either or both of them has or have a beneficial interest shall apply in relation to any property in which either or both of the parties to the agreement had a beneficial interest while the agreement was in force as they apply in relation to property in which either or both spouses has or have a beneficial interest.

(2) Where an agreement to marry is terminated, section 12 of the Married Women's Status Act, 1957, (which relates to the determination of questions between husband and wife as to property) shall apply, as if the parties to the agreement were married, to any dispute between them, or claim by one of them, in relation to property in which either or both had a beneficial interest while the agreement was in force."

Conveyancing Practice

It is the practice at the requisitions stage of a conveyance to ascertain whether the property in sale is affected by any of the foregoing provisions. Depending on the replies to the requisitions raised, the consent of the non-vendor party to the terminated agreement to marry may be required to be endorsed on the conveyance. The provisions – of which the most far-reaching in conveyancing practice is section 5(1) – are however relevant only infrequently. Therefore, the usual requirement at deed stage is simply a statutory declaration by the vendor to the effect that the provisions of the Family Law Act, 1981, do not affect the property in sale.

ℐ*Index*

AGENCY AND CONVEYANCING 183
AGENCY BY AUTHORITY 183
  Apparent Authority 184
  Express Authority 183
  Implied Authority 183
AGENCY BY RATIFICATION 184
AGENCY OF NECESSITY 186
AUCTIONEERS AND ESTATE AGENTS 198
CREATION OF AGENCY 183
DUTIES OF AN AGENT 186
  Accounts 188
  Act Personally 187
  Diligence and Skill 186
  Good Faith 187
  Obedience 186
RELATIONSHIP BETWEEN PRINCIPAL AND AGENT 186
RELATIONSHIP OF PRINCIPAL AND AGENT TO THIRD
PARTIES 191
  Agent's Participation in Third Party Contracts 192
  Miscellaneous Matters arising on Third Party Contracts 194
    Payments to Agent 194
    Principal styled as Agent 195
    Set-off 195
  Principal's Participation in Third Party Contracts 191
  Special Rules Regarding Participation in Third Party Contracts . 193
RIGHTS OF AN AGENT 188
  Commission 188
    Contract Overriding 188
    Contracts Prohibited by Statute 190
    Interpretation of Contract 188
    Quantum Meruit 190
    Sole and Exclusive Agents 189
  Indemnity 188
  Lien 190
  Stoppage in Transit 191
TERMINATION OF AGENCY 196
  Position of Third Parties on Termination of Agency 198
  Termination by Act of the Parties 196
    Agency coupled with Interest 197

Agency in Progress 197
Express Terms 196
Implied Terms 196
Termination by Operation of Law 197

CONSENTS REQUIRED UNDER THE LAND ACT, 1965 .... **161**
INTRODUCTION 161
SECTION 12, LAND ACT, 1965 161
   Exclusion from Section 12 of Certain Agricultural Land 162
   General Consent Procedure 162
   Vendor's Responsibility 162
SECTION 45, LAND ACT, 1965 164
   Exclusion from Consent Requirements of Certain Vestings 165
   Miscellaneous Provisions in the Section 168
   Non-application of Section 45 to Certain Land 164
   Purchaser's Responsibility 168
   Qualified Persons 165

CONTRACT OF SALE **128**
COMPLIANCE OF CONTRACT OF SALE WITH STATUTE
OF FRAUDS 129
   Analysis of the Requirements 129
   Consequences where a Contract of Sale does not comply with
   the Statute of Frauds 131
   Signature of Party to be Charged or of his Authorised Agent ... 130
   Written Agreement or Memorandum thereof in Writing 129
DISCHARGE OF THE CONTRACT 135
ENFORCEMENT OF THE CONTRACT OF SALE 135
   Contract distinguished from Agreement to Contract 136
   Sufficiency of the Written Details 137
   Suspensive Conditions 138
   The Requirement of Writing 137
RELATIONSHIP ARISING BETWEEN VENDOR AND
PURCHASER UNDER THE CONTRACT OF SALE 131
   Rights and Duties of the Purchaser 132
   Rights and Duties of the Vendor 132
      Damages 133
      Declaration 134
      Injunction 134
      Rescission 134
      Specific Performance 134
TYPES OF CONTRACT 128
   Formal Written Contract 128
   Open and Written Contract 129
   Verbal Contract 128

CO-OWNERSHIP **37**
CHARACTERISTICS 38
   Unity of interest 38

Unity of possession 38
Unity of time 39
Unity of title 39
CONSEQUENCES OF DIFFERENT TYPES OF CO-OWNERSHIP .. 40
Determination of co-ownership by Union 43
Partition 42
Severance 41
Survivorship 40
COPARCENARY 43
FAMILY HOME PROTECTION ACT, 1976 44
INTRODUCTION 37
JOINT TENANCY AND TENANCY IN COMMON 38
General 38
PREFERENCES FOR ONE FORM OF CO-OWNERSHIP
OVER ANOTHER 39
TENANCY BY ENTIRETIES 43

EASEMENTS AND PROFITS 85
ACQUISITION OF EASEMENTS 86
Express Grant or Reservation 87
Implied Grant or Reservation 87
Intention 88
Necessity 88
Prescription 89
Statute 92
Wheeldon v. Burrows 88
Common Law Prescription 89
Defences to Prescriptive Claims 91
Prescription under the Doctrine of the Lost Modern Grant 89
Statutory Prescription under the 1858 Act 90
Defences to Statutory Prescriptive Claims 91
General Defences 91
ACQUISITION OF PROFITS 97
Express Grant or Reservation 97
Implied Grant or Reservation 97
Prescription 97
Common Law 89
Lost Modern Grant 89
Statutory 90
EASEMENT DEFINED 85
EXTINGUISHMENT OF EASEMENTS 95
Express Release 95
Implied Release 95
Merger 96
Statute · 96
EXTINGUISHMENT OF PROFITS 95
PREREQUISITES TO EASEMENTS 85
PROFITS A PRENDRE 96
RELATIONSHIP BETWEEN DOMINANT AND SERVIENT OWNERS 94

THE EASEMENT OF LIGHT 92
   Acquisition 92
   Scope of Acquired Easement of light 93

FORM AND EFFECT OF A CONVEYANCE OF A FEE SIMPLE . 169
COVENANTS FOR TITLE 175
   Enforceability of the Covenants 176
   Operation of the Covenants 175
FORM OF A CONVEYANCE OF A FEE SIMPLE 169
   Acknowledgement and Undertaking 173
   Commencement and Date 170
   Consideration 171
   Covenants and Reservations 172
   Habendum 172
   Operative Words 172
   Parcels 172
   Parties 170
   Receipt Clause 171
   Recitals 170
   Statutory Certificates 173
   Testatum 171
   Testimonium and Attestation 174
MEANING OF CONVEYANCE 169
PRACTICE AFTER COMPLETION 177
   Mortgage by Purchaser to Lender 179
   Registration of Conveyance under Registry of Deeds System ... 177
THE DEED AS A CONVEYANCING INSTRUMENT 169

FREEHOLD ESTATES 6
BASE FEE 12
FEE SIMPLE 6
   Determinable and Conditional Fees Distinguished 9
   Determinable Fee Simple 8
   Fee Simple upon Condition Subsequent 8
FEE TAIL 10
INTRODUCTION 6
LIFE ESTATE 12
   Conventional Life Estates 13
   Legal Life Estates 13
   Transfer of Life Estates 13
RIGHTS OF HOLDER OF LIFE ESTATE 14
   Right of Alienation 14
   Rights of Enjoyment 14
      Emblements 15
      Fixtures 15
      Waste 14

FUTURE INTERESTS 45
INTRODUCTION 45

RULE AGAINST ACCUMULATION OF INCOME 63
RULE AGAINST PERPETUAL TRUSTS 61
   The Alienability Policy of the Common Law 61
   Rule against Perpetual Trusts 63
   The Perpetual Purpose Trust 62
RULES COVERING THE REMOTENESS OF VESTING OF
FUTURE INTERESTS 55
RULES GOVERNING THE VALIDITY OF LEGAL REMAINDERS . 53
RULE IN SHELLEY'S CASE 64
RULE IN WHITBY V. MITCHELL 56
THE RULE AGAINST PERPETUITIES 56
   Application of the Rule against Perpetuities to
   Various Types of Interests 61
   Application of the Rule to Gifts to Classes 59
   Effect of Invalidity of an Interest Under the Rule
   against Perpetuities 61
   Perpetuity Period 57
   Powers of Appointment and the Rule against Perpetuities 59
   Required Certainty of Vesting 59
   Validity of Appointed Interests 60
   Validity of the Power 60
   Vesting in Interest 58
TYPES OF FUTURE INTERESTS 47
   Executory Interests 48
   Remainders 47
   Reversions 47
VESTED AND CONTINGENT INTERESTS 46

IMPACT OF THE FAMILY HOME PROTECTION ACT, 1976,
AND THE FAMILY LAW ACT, 1981 245
FAMILY HOME PROTECTION ACT, 1976 245
   Certain Conveyances Void 245
   Conveyancing Practice 246
   Definitions 245
   Exceptions to the Rule in Section 3(1) 246
FAMILY LAW ACT, 1981 247
   Conveyancing Practice 248
   Relevant Provisions 247

LEASEHOLD INTERESTS 16
ALIENATION OF DEMISED PROPERTY 29
ALTERATIONS TO, AND IMPROVEMENTS OF,
DEMISED PROPERTY 29
CONTENTS OF THE CONTRACT 20
COVENANTS TO YIELD UP POSSESSION 30
DETERMINATION OF LEASEHOLD INTERESTS 31
   Effluxion of Time 31
   Notice to Quit 31
   Surrender 32

Forfeiture 33
  Breach of Condition 34
  Breach of Covenant Supported by Re-Entry Clause or
  Forfeiture Clause 34
  Disclaimer of Title 34
  Reliefs against Forfeiture 35
  Restriction on Forfeiture 34
  Merger 32
  Notice to Quit 31
  Surrender 32
  Statutory Ejectment 35
FORMALITIES NECESSARY IN CREATING
THE RELATIONSHIP 18
INSURANCE OF DEMISED PROPERTY 29
INTRODUCTION 16
LANDLORD'S OBLIGATIONS TO TENANT 30
RELATIONSHIP OF LANDLORD AND TENANT BASED ON
CONTRACT 17
RENT 24
  Amount Payable 24
  Landlord's Remedies for the Recovery of Rent 26
  Rent Payable 25
  Salvage Payments 26
REPAIRS 26
  Determination of the Extent of Repairing Liability 28
  Landlord's Liability 27
  Tenant's Liability 27
TYPES OF LEASEHOLD INTEREST 20
  Fixed Terms 20
  Periodic Tenancies 22
  Renewable Leases and Fee Farm Grants 21
  Tenancies at Sufferance 23
  Tenancies at Will 22
  Tenancies by Estoppel 23
USER OF DEMISED PROPERTY 28

MORTGAGES 65
CREATION OF MORTGAGES 68
EQUITABLE MORTGAGES 70
  Agreement to Create a Legal Mortgage 70
  Deposit of Title Deeds as Security for a Loan 70
  Mortgage of an Equitable Interest in Property 71
  Supplementary Points on the Creation of Mortgages 71
IMPORTANCE OF THE MORTGAGE IN CONVEYANCING
PRACTICE 65
  Ability to Repay 66
  Value of the Property Available as Security 67
JUDGEMENT MORTGAGES 83
LEGAL MORTGAGES 68

Unregistered Freehold 68
Unregistered Leasehold 69
MORTGAGE DEFINED 65
MORTGAGEE'S RIGHTS, POWERS AND REMEDIES 72
    Miscellaneous Rights 80
    Right to Accept Surrenders of leases 77
    Right to Appoint a Receiver 76
    Right to Consolidate 79
    Right to Fixtures 79
    Right to Grant Leases 77
    Right to Insure 78
    Right to Possession 73
    Right to Possession of Title Deeds 78
    Right to Sell 74
    Right to Stay Out of Mortgagor's Bankruptcy Proceedings 80
    Rights to Sue on the Personal Covenant for Repayment 72
    Right to Tack Further Advances 80
MORTGAGOR'S RIGHTS, POWERS AND REMEDIES 80
    Miscellaneous Rights 82
    Right to Redeem 80
    Right to the Rent and Profits of the Mortgaged Property 82
PRIORITY BETWEEN MORTGAGES 82
    Doctrine of Tacking 83
    Impact of the Registry Act, 1707 83
    Unregistered Mortgages 82

NATURE OF REAL PROPERTY 3
DIFFERENCES ARISING FROM THE DISTINCTION
BETWEEN REAL AND PERSONAL PROPERTY 4
REAL PROPERTY AND PERSONAL PROPERTY CONTRASTED ... 3
SPECIAL CLASSIFICATION OF LEASEHOLDS 3
TENURE 4

REGISTRATION OF DEEDS 214
INTRODUCTION 214
METHOD OF REGISTRATION 215
RECORDS MAINTAINED IN THE REGISTRY OF DEEDS 217
REGISTRABLE DOCUMENTS 215
RULES GOVERNING PRIORITIES 216
    Conflict between Registered and Unregistered Deeds 216
    Conflict between Registered Deeds as between Themselves .. 217
    Conflict between Registered Deeds where one of them
    is Voluntary 217
    Conflict between Unregistered or Unregistrable Deeds 217
SEARCHES IN THE REGISTRY OF DEEDS 218
The Period of Search 219
Types of Search 218

REGISTRATION OF TITLE 220
CAUTIONS AND INHIBITIONS 231
CLASSES OF OWNERSHIP IN THE LAND REGISTRY 223
CLASSES OF TITLE THAT MAY BE REGISTERED 224
   Conversion of Title 227
   Four Classes of Leasehold Title 225
   Three Classes of Freehold Title 224
COMPULSORY REGISTRATION 228
CONCLUSIVENESS OF THE REGISTER 227
FIRST REGISTRATION 230
INTRODUCTION 220
LAND CERTIFICATE 234
LAND REGISTRY OFFICES AND REGISTERS 221
   Land Registry Offices 221
   Registers 222
LAND REGISTRY SEARCHES 233
LAND REGISTRY TRANSFERS 230

SETTLED LAND ACTS 203
INTRODUCTION 203
OVERREACHING 211
   Binding Rights created under the Settlement 213
   Certain Legal Mortgages 212
   Prior Legal Estates 212
POWERS OF A TENANT FOR LIFE 205
   Power to Effect Improvements 208
   Power to Grant Options 207
   Power to Mortgage 207
   Power to Grant Leases 205
   Powers of Sale and Exchange 205
SETTLED LAND DEFINED 204
TENANT FOR LIFE 205
TRUSTEES OF THE SETTLEMENT 208
   Functions of Trustees 210
   Identification of the Trustees 208

STAGES IN A CONVEYANCE 123
   First Stage: From Preliminary Negotiations to Contract 123
   Fourth Stage: After Closing 126
   Introduction 123
   Second Stage: From Contract to Closing 124
   Third Stage: Closing 126

STAMP DUTY 237
AD VALOREM DUTY 237
   Chattels 240
   Leases 239
   Mortgages, Bonds, Debentures and Covenants 239
   Settlements 240

Transactions between Related Persons 238
Transfers between Associated Companies 239
Voluntary Dispositions Inter Vivos 238
FIXED RATE OF DUTY 240
GENERAL EXEMPTIONS FROM STAMP DUTY 241
INTRODUCTION 237

STANDARD CONTRACT OF SALE 139
CONSENT OF SPOUSE AND MEMORANDUM OF
AGREEMENT 139
GENERAL CONDITIONS OF SALE 143
INTRODUCTION 139
PARTICULARS AND TENURE 140
PRELIMINARY 139
SCHEDULES OF DOCUMENTS AND SEARCHES 141
SPECIAL CONDITIONS 142

**SUBSIDIARY SEARCHES IN CONVEYANCING
TRANSACTIONS** 242
FREEHOLD PROPERTY 242
  Bankruptcy Search 242
  Lis Pendens Search 242
  Planning Search 243
  Search on the Judgements Register 243
INTRODUCTION 242
LEASEHOLD PROPERTY 243
  Sheriffs Office Search 243
SUBSIDIARY SEARCHES FOR BOTH FREEHOLD AND
LEASEHOLD PROPERTY 244
  A Companies' Office Search 244
  District Court Office Search 244
  Search of Friendly Societies Register 244

SUCCESSION 99
ADVANCEMENTS 108
BENEFICIAL DEVOLUTION OF ALL PROPERTY ON
INTESTACY AFTER THE SUCCESSION ACT 109
  Introduction 109
  Rules for Distribution of All Property on Intestacy
  After the Succession Act 110
BENEFICIAL DEVOLUTION OF PERSONALTY ON
INTESTACY BEFORE THE SUCCESSION ACT 105
  Rules for ascertaining the Next-Of-Kin Who Should Benefit 106
BENEFICIAL DEVOLUTION OF REALTY ON INTESTACY
BEFORE THE SUCCESSION ACT 100
  Ancestors and Collaterals 101
  Ascertainment of Heir 101
Curtesy and Dower 102
  Curtesy 102

Dower 103
Issue 101
Relatives of the Half Blood 102
Trace from last Purchaser 101
DETERMINING DEGREES OF KINSHIP 103
Collaterals 104
Descendants and Ancestors 104
Inheritance by Representation 105
INTESTATES' ESTATE ACTS, 1890 and 1954 108
INTRODUCTION 99
POWER OF TESTATION 115
Advancements to be taken into Account 116
"Forced Share" Provisions 118
Gifts to an Attesting Witness, or to the Spouse of Such
a Witness, are Void 117
Provision for Children 119
Right of Surviving Spouse to Appropriation of Dwelling
and Household Chattels 116
VARIOUS ASPECTS OF THE LAW RELATING TO WILLS 111
Essentials of the Validity of Wills 113
Animus Testandi 113
Compliance with Statutory Formalities 113
Testator's Capacity 113
Introduction 111
Revival of Wills 115
Revocation of Wills 114
By a Document 114
By Actual Destruction 114
By Marriage 114

TITLE TO BE SHOWN UNDER AN OPEN CONTRACT 115
BAD ROOTS OF TITLE. VENDOR'S DUTY OF DISCLOSURE 160
INTRODUCTION 155
SEARCHING TITLE TO UNREGISTERED FREEHOLD
PROPERTY 155
Roots of Title 156
The period of Title 155
Doubtful Roots of Title 157
Good Roots of Title 156
SEARCHING TITLE TO UNREGISTERED LEASEHOLD
PROPERTY 157
Period of Title 157
Statutory Provisions that may Restrict the Investigation 158
Summary of Task in Investigation of Title to
Unregistered Leasehold Property 158